Bloom's BioCritiques

Bloom's BioCritiques

TENNESSEE WILLIAMS

Edited and with an introduction by
Harold Bloom
Sterling Professor of the Humanities
Yale University

CHELSEA HOUSE
PUBLISHERS
A Haights Cross Communications Company
Philadelphia

Printed and bound in the United States of America

10 9 8 7 6 5 4 3 2 1

Library of Congress Cataloging-in-Publication Data

Chelsea House Publishers
1974 Sproul Road, Suite 400
Broomall, PA 19008-0914

http://www.chelseahouse.com

Contributing editor: Aimee LaBrie

Cover design by Keith Trego

Cover: Baldwin H. Ward & Kathryn C. Ward/CORBIS

Layout by EJB Publishing Services

CONTENTS

User's Guide

These volumes are designed to introduce the reader to the life and work of the world's literary masters. Each volume begins with Harold Bloom's essay "The Work in the Writer" and a volume-specific introduction also written by Professor Bloom. Following these unique introductions is an engaging biography that discusses the major life events and important literary accomplishments of the author under consideration.

Furthermore, each volume includes an original critique that not only traces the themes, symbols, and ideas apparent in the author's works, but strives to put those works into a cultural and historical perspective. In addition to the original critique is a brief selection of significant critical essays previously published on the author and his or her works followed by a concise and informative chronology of the writer's life. Finally, each volume concludes with a bibliography of the writer's works, a list of additional readings, and an index of important themes and ideas.

HAROLD BLOOM

The Work in the Writer

Literary biography found its masterpiece in James Boswell's *Life of Samuel Johnson*. Boswell, when he treated Johnson's writings, implicitly commented upon Johnson as found in his work, even as in the great critic's life. Modern instances of literary biography, such as Richard Ellmann's lives of W. B. Yeats, James Joyce, and Oscar Wilde, essentially follow in Boswell's pattern.

That the writer somehow is in the work, we need not doubt, though with William Shakespeare, writer-of-writers, we almost always need to rely upon pure surmise. The exquisite rancidities of the Problem Plays or Dark Comedies seem to express an extraordinary estrangement of Shakespeare from himself. When we read or attend *Troilus and Cressida* and *Measure for Measure*, we may be startled by particular speeches of Ulysses in the first play, or of Vincentio in the second. These speeches, of Ulysses upon hierarchy or upon time, or of Duke Vincentio upon death, are too strong either for their contexts or for the characters of their speakers. The same phenomenon occurs with Parolles, the military impostor of *All's Well That Ends Well*. Utterly disgraced, he nevertheless affirms: "Simply the thing I am/Shall make me live."

In Shakespeare, more even than in his peers, Dante and Cervantes, meaning always starts itself again through excess or overflow. The strongest of Shakespeare's creatures—Falstaff, Hamlet, Iago, Lear, Cleopatra—have an exuberance that is fiercer than their plays can contain. If Ben Jonson was at all correct in his complaint that "Shakespeare wanted art," it could have been only in a sense that he may not have intended. Where do the personalities of Falstaff or Hamlet touch a limit? What was it in Shakespeare that made the two parts of *Henry IV* and *Hamlet* into "plays unlimited"? Neither Falstaff nor Hamlet will be stopped: their wit, their beautiful, laughing speech, their intensity of being—all these are virtually infinite.

In what ways do Falstaff and Hamlet manifest the writer in the work? Evidently, we can never know, or know enough to answer with any authority. But what would happen if we reversed the question, and asked: How did the work form the writer, Shakespeare?

Of Shakespeare's inwardness, his biography tells us nothing. And yet, to an astonishing extent, Shakespeare created our inwardness. At the least, we can speculate that Shakespeare so lived his life as to conceal the depths of his nature, particularly as he rather prematurely aged. We do not have Shakespeare on Shakespeare, as any good reader of the Sonnets comes to realize: they do not constitute a key that unlocks his heart. No sequence of sonnets could be less confessional or more powerfully detached from the poet's self.

The German poet and universal genius, Goethe, affords a superb contrast to Shakespeare. Of Goethe's life, we know more than everything; I wonder sometimes if we know as much about Napoleon or Freud or any other human being who ever has lived, as we know about Goethe. Everywhere, we can find Goethe in his work, so much so that Goethe seems to crowd the writing out, just as Byron and Oscar Wilde seem to usurp their own literary accomplishments. Goethe, cunning beyond measure, nevertheless invested a rival exuberance in his greatest works that could match his personal charisma. The sublime outrageousness of the Second Part of *Faust*, or of the greater lyric and meditative poems, form a Counter-Sublime to Goethe's own daemonic intensity.

Goethe was fascinated by the daemonic in himself; we can doubt that Shakespeare had any such interests. Evidently, Shakespeare abandoned his acting career just before he composed *Measure for Measure* and *Othello*. I surmise that the egregious interventions by Vincentio and Iago displace the actor's energies into a new kind of mischief-making, a fresh opening to a subtler playwriting-within-the-play.

But what had opened Shakespeare to this new awareness? The answer is the work in the writer, *Hamlet* in Shakespeare. One can go further: it was not so much the play, *Hamlet*, as the character Hamlet, who changed Shakespeare's art forever.

Hamlet's personality is so large and varied that it rivals Goethe's own. Ironically Goethe's Faust, his Hamlet, has no personality at all, and is as colorless as Shakespeare himself seems to have chosen to be. Yet nothing could be more colorful than the Second Part of *Faust*, which is peopled by an astonishing array of monsters, grotesque devils, and classical ghosts.

A contrast between Shakespeare and Goethe demonstrates that in each—but in very different ways—we can better find the work in the person, than we can discover that banal entity, the person in the work. Goethe to many of his contemporaries, seemed to be a mortal god. Shakespeare, so far as we know, seemed an affable, rather ordinary fellow, who aged early and became somewhat withdrawn. Yet Faust, though Mephistopheles battles for his soul, is hardly worth the trouble unless you take him as an idea and not as a person. Hamlet is nearly every-idea-in-one, but he is precisely a personality and a person.

Would Hamlet be so astonishingly persuasive if his father's ghost did not haunt him? Falstaff is more alive than Prince Hal, who says that the devil haunts him in the shape of an old fat man. Three years before composing the final *Hamlet*, Shakespeare invented Falstaff, who then never ceased to haunt his creator. Falstaff and Hamlet may be said to best represent the work in the writer, because their influence upon Shakespeare was prodigious. W.H. Auden accurately observed that Falstaff possesses infinite energy: never tired, never bored, and absolutely both witty and happy until Hal's rejection destroys him. Hamlet too has infinite energy, but in him it is more curse than blessing.

Falstaff and Hamlet can be said to occupy the roles in Shakespeare's invented world that Sancho Panza and Don Quixote possess in Cervantes's. Shakespeare's plays from 1610 on (starting with *Twelfth Night*) are thus analogous to the Second Part of Cervantes's epic novel. Sancho and the Don overtly jostle Cervantes for authorship in the Second Part, even as Cervantes battles against the impostor who has pirated a continuation of his work. As a dramatist, Shakespeare manifests the work in the writer more indirectly. Falstaff's prose genius is revived in the scapegoating of Malvolio by Maria and Sir Toby Belch, while Falstaff's darker insights are developed by Feste's melancholic wit. Hamlet's intellectual resourcefulness, already deadly, becomes poisonous in Iago and in Edmund. Yet we have not crossed into the deeper abysses of the work in the writer in later Shakespeare.

No fictive character, before or since, is Falstaff's equal in self-trust. Sir John, whose delight in himself is contagious, has total confidence both in his self-awareness and in the resources of his language. Hamlet, whose self is as strong, and whose language is as copious, nevertheless distrusts both the self and language. Later Shakespeare is, as it were, much under the influence both of Falstaff and of Hamlet, but they tug him in opposite directions. Shakespeare's own copiousness of language is well-nigh incredible: a vocabulary in excess of twenty-one thousand words, almost eighteen hundred of which he coined himself. And of his word-hoard, nearly half are used only once each, as though the perfect setting for each had been found, and need not be repeated. Love for language and faith in language are Falstaffian attributes. Hamlet will darken both that love and that faith in Shakespeare, and perhaps the Sonnets can best be read as Falstaff and Hamlet counterpointing against one another.

Can we surmise how aware Shakespeare was of Falstaff and Hamlet, once they had played themselves into existence? *Henry IV, Part I* appeared in six quarto editions during Shakespeare's lifetime; *Hamlet* possibly had four. Falstaff and Hamlet were played again and again at the Globe, but Shakespeare knew also that they were being read, and he must have had contact with some of those readers. What would it have been like to discuss Falstaff or Hamlet with one of their early readers (presumably also part of their audience at the Globe), if you were the creator of such demiurges? The question would seem nonsensical to most Shakespeare scholars, but then these days they tend to be either ideologues or moldy figs. How can we recover the uncanniness of Falstaff and of Hamlet, when they now have become so familiar?

A writer's influence upon himself is an unexplored problem in criticism, but such an influence is never free from anxieties. The biocritical problem (which this series attempts to explore) can be divided into two areas, difficult to disengage fully. Accomplished works affect the author's life, and also affect her subsequent writings. It is simpler for me to surmise the effect of *Mrs. Dalloway* and *To the Lighthouse* upon Woolf's late *Between the Acts*, than it is to relate Clarissa Dalloway's suicide and Lily Briscoe's capable endurance in art to the tragic death and complex life of Virginia Woolf.

There are writers whose lives were so vivid that they seem sometimes to obscure the literary achievement: Byron, Wilde, Malraux, Hemingway. But most major Western writers do not live that exuberantly, and the greatest of all, Shakespeare, sometimes appears to have adopted the personal mask of colorlessness. And yet there are heroes of literature who struggled titanically with their own eras—Tolstoy, Milton, Victor Hugo—who nevertheless matter more for their works than their lives.

There are great figures—Emily Dickinson, Wallace Stevens, Willa Cather—who seem to have had so little of the full intensity of life when compared to the vitality of their work, that we might almost speak of the work in the work, rather than even of the work in a person. Emily Brontë might well be the extreme instance of such a visionary, surpassing William Blake in that one regard.

I conclude this general introduction to a series of literary bio-critiques by stating a tentative formula or principle for gauging the many ways in which the work influences the person and her subsequent, later work. Our influence upon ourselves is always related to the Shakespearean invention of self-overhearing, which I have written about in several other contexts. Life, as well as poetry and prose, is overheard rather than simply heard. The writer listens to herself as though she were somebody else, and the will to change begins to operate. The forces that live in us include the prior work we have done, and the dreams and waking visions that evade our dismissals.

HAROLD BLOOM

Introduction

The American theater, by the common estimate of its most eminent critics, touches an initial strength with Eugene O'Neill, and then proceeds to the more varied excellences of Thornton Wilder, Tennessee Williams, Arthur Miller, Edward Albee, and Sam Shepard. That sequence is clearly problematical, and becomes even more worrisome when we move from playwrights to plays. Which are our dramatic works that matter most? *Long Day's Journey Into Night*, certainly; perhaps *The Iceman Cometh*; evidently *A Streetcar Named Desire* and *Death of a Salesman*; perhaps again *The Skin of Our Teeth* and *The Zoo Story*—it is not God's plenty. And I will venture the speculation that our drama palpably is not yet literary enough. By this I do not just mean that O'Neill writes very badly, or Miller very badly; they do, but so did Dreiser, and *Sister Carrie* and *An American Tragedy* prevail nevertheless. Nor do I wish to be an American Matthew Arnold (whom I loathe above all other critics) and proclaim that our dramatists simply have not known enough. They know more than enough, and that is part of the trouble.

Literary tradition, as I have come to understand it, masks the agon between past and present as a benign relationship, whether personal or societal. The actual transferences between the force of the literary past and the potential of writing in the present tend to be darker, even if they do not always or altogether follow the defensive patterns of what Sigmund Freud called "family romances." Whether or not an

1

ambivalence, however repressed, towards the past's force is felt by the new writer and is manifested in his work seems to depend entirely upon the ambition and power of the oncoming artist. If he aspires after strength, and can attain it, then he must struggle with both a positive and a negative transference, false connections because necessarily imagined ones, between a composite precursor and himself. His principal resource in that agon will be his own native gift for interpretation, or as I am inclined to call it, strong misreading. Revising his precursor, he will create himself, make himself into a kind of changeling, and so he will become, in an illusory but highly pragmatic way, his own father.

The most literary of our major dramatists, and clearly I mean "literary" in a precisely descriptive sense, neither pejorative nor eulogistic, was Tennessee Williams. Wilder, with his intimate connections to *Finnegans Wake* and Gertrude Stein, might seem to dispute this placement, and Wilder was certainly more literate than Williams. But Wilder had a benign relation to his crucial precursor, Joyce, and did not aspire after a destructive strength. Williams did, and suffered the fate he prophesied and desired; the strength destroyed his later work, and his later life, and thus joined itself to the American tradition of self-destructive genius. Williams truly had one precursor only: Hart Crane, the greatest of our lyrical poets, after Whitman and Dickinson, and the most self-destructive figure in our national literature, surpassing all others in this, as in so many regards.

Williams asserted he had other precursors also: D. H. Lawrence, and Chekhov in the drama. These were outward influences, and benefited Williams well enough, but they were essentially formal, and so not the personal and societal family romance of authentic poetic influence. Hart Crane made Williams into more of a dramatic lyrist, though writing in prose, than the lyrical dramatist that Williams is supposed to have been. Though this influence—perhaps more nearly an identification—helped form *The Glass Menagerie* and (less overtly) *A Streetcar Named Desire*, and in a lesser mode *Summer and Smoke* and *Suddenly Last Summer*, it also led to such disasters of misplaced lyricism as the dreadful *Camino Real* and the dreary *The Night of the Iguana*. (*Cat on a Hot Tin Roof*, one of Williams's best plays, does not seem to me to show any influence of Crane.) Williams's long aesthetic decline covered thirty years, from 1953 to 1983, and reflected the sorrows of a seer who, by his early forties, had outlived his own vision. Hart Crane, self-slain at thirty-two, had set for Williams a High Romantic paradigm that helped cause Williams, his heart as dry as summer dust, to burn to the socket.

Ever since I first fell in love with Hart Crane's poetry, almost sixty years ago, I have wondered what the poet of *The Bridge* and "The Broken Tower" would have accomplished, had he not killed himself. One doesn't see Crane burning out; he was poetically strongest at the very end, despite his despair. Williams identified his own art, and his own despair, with Crane's. Tom Wingfield, Blanche DuBois, and even Sebastian Venable are closer to self-portraits than they are depictions of Hart Crane, but crucial images of Crane's poetry intricately fuse into Williams's visions of himself. One of the oddities of *Suddenly Last Summer* is that Catharine is far closer to an accurate inner portrait of Hart Crane than is the poet Sebastian Venable, who lacks Crane's honesty and courage. Williams's obsession with Crane twists *Suddenly Last Summer* askew, and should not prevent us from seeing that Williams's self-hatred dominates the depiction of Sebastian.

The aesthetic vocation and homosexual identity are difficult to distinguish both in Crane and in Williams, though both poet and playwright develop stratagems, rhetorical and cognitive, that enrich this difficulty without reducing it to case histories. Tom Wingfield's calling will become Williams's, though *The Glass Menagerie* presents Wingfield's quest as a flight away from the family romance, the incestuous images of the mother and the sister. Blanche Du Bois, much closer to Williams himself, risks the playwright's masochistic self-parody, and yet her defeat has considerable aesthetic dignity. More effective on stage than in print, her personality is a touch too wistful to earn the great epitaph from Crane's "The Broken Tower" that Williams insists upon employing:

> And so it was I entered the broken world
> To trace the visionary company of love, its voice
> An instant in the wind (I know not whither hurled)
> But not for long to hold each desperate choice.

Williams, in his *Memoirs*, haunted as always by Hart Crane, refers to his precursor as "a tremendous and yet fragile artist," and then associates both himself and Blanche with the fate of Crane, a suicide by drowning in the Caribbean:

I am as much of an hysteric as ... Blanche; a codicil to my will
provides for the disposition of my body in this way. "Sewn up
in a clean white sack and dropped over board, twelve hours
north of Havana, so that my bones may rest not too far from
those of Hart Crane ..."

At the conclusion of *Memoirs*, Williams again associated Crane
both with his own vocation and his own limitations, following Crane
even in an identification with the young Rimbaud:

A poet such as the young Rimbaud is the only writer of
whom I can think, at this moment, who could escape from
words into the sensations of being, through his youth,
turbulent with revolution, permitted articulation by nights of
absinthe. And of course there is Hart Crane. Both of these
poets touched fire that burned them alive. And perhaps it is
only through self-immolation of such a nature that we living
beings can offer to you the entire truth of ourselves within
the reasonable boundaries of a book.

For all his gifts, Williams was a far more flawed artist than Crane,
whose imaginative heroism was beyond anything Williams could ever
attain.

NORMA JEAN LUTZ

Biography of Tennessee Williams

CREATING *THE GLASS MENAGERIE*

At Chicago's Union Station, on December 17, 1944, the cast of *The Glass Menagerie* assembled with only two weeks left to prepare for the play's debut. The motley group milling on the platform gave no sign of a common purpose; most of the actors barely knew one another. And when the playwright, Thomas Lanier "Tennessee" Williams, returned to the train to retrieve an item he'd left behind, he emerged to find that almost everyone had already left for the hotel; only the actor who would star in the production, Laurette Taylor, remained. Williams called out to her, and she replied; this encounter at Union Station was the start of an enduring friendship. "Then and there," Williams would later recall, "we joined forces."

Taylor hailed a cab for them "with an imperious wave of her ungloved hand, hesitation all gone as she sprang like a tiger out of her cloud of softness." Her confidence would be vital to the production's success or failure, and it was as important to Taylor that the play succeed as it was to Williams. Earlier in her career, Taylor had been known as one of America's greatest actors; her successes in productions of *Peg o' My Heart* and *Outward Bound* had been brilliant, but all such coups had taken place a decade before. She had been absent from the stage for many years by 1944, and she was rumored to have become an alcoholic. Eddie Dowling, the director of the play and also one of its actors, had called the sixty-year-old Taylor out of retirement to play the role of Amanda Wingfield. Taylor had stayed up most of the night reading the script to *The Glass Menagerie*, and by the next morning she'd recognized it as the perfect opportunity to reestablish herself in the public eye.

Indeed, almost everyone who read the script had liked it. Williams' agent, Audrey Wood, had easily persuaded Dowling to produce the play, and Dowling decided to star in the production as well, taking on the role of Tom Wingfield. Julie Haydon—who had played in more than twenty films in the 1930s and provided the screams for Fay Wray in *King Kong* (1933)—agreed to originate the role of the crippled daughter, Laura. The relatively inexperienced Anthony Ross would play Jim O'Connor, "the gentleman caller."

Dowling secured financial backing for the production from a Wall Street broker named Louis J. Singer. Singer was fascinated with the theater, but he had little or no working knowledge of what went into the production of a play—so the budget was tight. The troupe had no access to a theater in New York; rehearsals were held in hotel rooms and apartments, even in Dowling's office. During rehearsals, Williams retreated to his childhood home in St. Louis, hoping to distance himself from the cast; he found actors intimidating and, moreover, dreaded the onslaught of the changes they would want to make to his script.

When the company left New York for the Chicago show, its members asked Williams to join them, as they very much wanted the author to be on hand for the full-scale rehearsals there. These rehearsals were often chaotic, and they frequently led to personality conflicts. Taylor felt from the outset that Dowling was far too old to play her son, and her temper flared as the two bickered. Taylor hadn't memorized many of her lines or practiced the Southern accent called for in her role; Williams remarked that she made the play sound like "The Aunt Jemima Pancake Hour." To further complicate matters, Chicago's Civic Theater was an inconvenient distance from the city's theater district; there was no budget for advertising, and the theater's sound system was crude and ineffective.

As the problems continued to mount, Louis Singer grew increasingly upset. Doubting the play's commercial appeal, he called a meeting and told the group that the script should be changed to end happily. Neither Dowling nor Williams uttered a word in defense of the original, but Margo Jones, "the Texas Tornado," a friend who would also become the play's co-director, objected vehemently, and she warned the financier that if the ending were changed she'd report his "wire-pulling" to every art critic in Chicago. The play's ending remained as it was.

Still, although Singer had backed down on changing the ending, he continued to complain about every expense. In a letter to Audrey Wood back in New York, Jones related that a lack of funds compelled them to sew some of their own costumes; Williams himself contributed $10 for one of the dresses, a week's pay for him at the time. And this was not the extent of the production's troubles; Paul Bowles, who scored the music for the play, remembered flying to Chicago through a terrible blizzard for a dress rehearsal, only to find that the theater was frigid and Taylor had again started drinking. Despite all this, though, a specially scheduled matinee was staged successfully on Christmas afternoon, for an audience of 400 uniformed members of another touring company. Also in the matinee audience was Williams' mother, Edwina, who had traveled by train from St. Louis alone, to attend.

By now, many members of the company had begun to grasp Taylor's method for assuming the role of the mother in the play. She had learned her "inner search" technique of characterization from her late husband, Hartley Manners, who had been her coach for many years. With little regard for how the troupe felt or how she made them suffer, her technique was to observe how the other players interacted with her character, after which she would "soak" herself in the facets that would be revealed by these exchanges. To solve the problem of Amanda's Southern accent, she imitated Williams himself. With all of the pieces in place, she assumed her character, and the effect was so overwhelming that many of the crew wept at her first rehearsal, including the young playwright himself. Later Williams summarized her performance with admiration: "She was continually working on her part, putting in little things and taking them out—almost every night in Chicago there was something new, but she never disturbed the central characterization. Everything she did was absolutely in character."

On opening night—December 26, 1944—Chicago was again in the grip of a blizzard. In her memoirs, Edwina Williams described her own arrival: "[E]verything seemed to be against the play, even the weather. The streets were so ice-laden we could not find a taxi to take us to the Civic Theater and had to walk. The gale blowing off Lake Michigan literally hurled us through the theatre door." The crowd that braved the storm by no means filled the theater.

When the curtain fell all was quiet, and Williams' mother thought that the audience had not liked the piece; but then the scant audience burst into sustained applause. Although the initial reception of the play was good, its success remained dubious, for its total take in the first week was a mere $3,670. Singer was ready to close the production down. Two Chicago critics, however, the *Tribune*'s Claudia Cassidy and the *Herald-American*'s Ashton Stevens, continued to attend, night after night; both wrote glowing reviews in their columns, and soon other reviewers followed suit. They reminded Chicago readers of past complaints about the low-quality second-string road shows that regularly appeared in their city, and they urged readers to support something truly extraordinary.

Their efforts achieved the desired result, and there was no premature closing. By the third week, calls were coming in regularly for group and individual tickets, and the house was packed every night. Soon the play was grossing $15,000 weekly, almost five times the take of its first week. Williams' abruptly found himself with $1,000, the first real money he had earned in all his years of sacrifice and diligence. Williams had spent most of his adult life working menial jobs, going hungry, and sometimes wandering the streets, homeless, but now those days appeared to be over. And although he remained in awe of Laurette Taylor, the two eventually became close friends. The praise she received for her performance, she graciously turned back to that "nice little guy," reminding people it was his lines that lent to the play its power and beauty. Before the production closed in Chicago, many Hollywood stars stopped off to see it on their way to New York—including Helen Hayes, Katherine Hepburn, Raymond Massey, and Gregory Peck. Some of Williams' classmates from Iowa attended, too, in honor of their friend.

By now, the front-office dilemma had become deciding how long to keep the show in Chicago and which New York offer to accept. Word of the success of the play had traveled quickly to Broadway, and several theaters waited with open arms. The Playhouse Theatre was chosen, and *The Glass Menagerie* was scheduled to open in New York on March 31, 1945.

But Laurette Taylor's health now seemed to be failing. During dress rehearsals, she was enervated and nauseated, and she seldom made it through more than one scene before pleading illness and taking leave of the stage. This routine went on for several days, and as opening night approached, the entire cast wondered whether she would be able to perform at all; and the aged Taylor did require the help of two people to reach the stage come showtime. Still, once the curtain rose and the lights came up, Taylor was in top form. At the play's end, the cast took a whopping 24 curtain calls. There were numerous cries for the author, too, who, with a boyish crewcut and a button missing from his suit coat, was at last persuaded to take the stage.

Within days, the lines outside the Playhouse were long and theatergoers were purchasing tickets weeks in advance. The cast put on 563 performances during the play's initial run in New York, with Taylor playing the role of Amanda until she became too ill to continue. Also during its New York run, it was voted the year's best play by the New York Drama Critics' Circle, in addition to garnering the Donaldson Award from the magazine *Billboard* and the Sidney Howard Memorial Award from the Playwrights Company, a major theatrical organization founded in 1937 by five luminaries, including the legendary Max Anderson. Williams' play was a hit now, and he was famous.

Laurette Taylor died in 1946. Williams wrote a penetrating tribute to her for *The New York Times*, the closing paragraph of which hints at Williams' vision of his relationship with the world of the theater:

> I feel now—as I have always felt—that a whole career of writing for the theatre is rewarded enough by having created one good part for a great actress. Having created a part for Laurette Taylor is a reward I find sufficient for all the effort that went before and any that may come after.

OPENING SCENES

One route to an understanding of Tennessee Williams' unique artistry, of the relationship between his work and his life, is through the strongest influence on his childhood: that of his family. Williams' grandfather, Walter Edwin Dakin, was born in southwestern Ohio in 1857. One of six sons born to Dr. Edwin Francis Dakin, Walter was confirmed at Saint Mary's Episcopal Church in Waynesville, where he later served as a deacon. Although he was named for his father, Walter did not follow in his father's footsteps professionally, for his own inclination was more toward the ministry than toward medicine. In fact, he saw *both* fields as impractical, and he later studied business and finance at Eastman College in Poughkeepsie, New York. On completing college, he returned to Ohio, where he was married.

Walter Dakin's wife, Rosina Otte, was the daughter of a German emigrant who, since his arrival in the U.S. from Hanover, had developed a substantial tailoring business that would remain in the family for generations. The Ottes were Lutheran, but the Otte children had been educated at a Roman Catholic school, after which Rose had studied at Cincinnati's famous Conservatory of Music, developing a passion for music that would remain with her throughout her life. Her engagement to Dakin followed her return from the Conservatory and a brief courtship; they were married in 1883. Rose's parents had hoped she would marry into a more affluent family, but they soon accepted Walter with great warmth. A year later, on August 19, 1884, Edwina Estelle Dakin was born to the new couple—their only child, and Tennessee Williams' mother.

When Rose's parents decided to leave Ohio, the Dakins went along, settling at last on a farm east of Chattanooga, Tennessee. Walter took a position as superintendent of the Shelbyville Female Institute, a school for girls, located halfway between Nashville and Chattanooga. The Institute offered to Walter both employment and accommodation and to Rose the opportunity to teach music and give piano concerts; some of Edwina's earliest memories were of seeing her mother sweep elegantly across the stage to be seated at the piano. The small house on the Institute's campus was the Dakins' first home away from the extended family.

They later moved to Tullahoma, Tennessee, where Walter became a regular reader at an Episcopal church—apparently with some success, for the minister asked whether he had considered, or would consider, studying for the ministry. Walter quickly replied that he was interested in becoming a minister, and the decision was made. Rose supported her husband's project by taking on extra music students and sewing assignments. Walter did become a minister, and afterward the Dakins traveled, visiting small, failing churches in the hope of breathing new life into them. This kept the family moving from place to place, but because the couple had become so popular to people in the church community, the transitions were relatively painless. As they moved through the South, Edwina, though of course not a true Southerner, quickly adopted the folkways of the South, even developing a soft, slurring accent that she would retain to her last days.

Edwina's was a peaceful and supportive childhood, not particularly marked by discord. She would later regret her inability to provide the same for her own children; "If there is one time in life a person ought to be free from fear," she wrote in her memoirs, "it is when he is growing up."

Edwina attended Wittenberg College—a junior college—and subsequently was offered a scholarship to Harcourt Place Seminary, where she spent three years and, harboring a secret desire to become a stage actor, became involved in a number of theatrical projects. After her graduation from Wittenberg, the Dakins relocated several times, landing at last in Natchez and then in Columbus, Mississippi; the genteel codes and customs of the Old South were still followed closely there, and Edwina felt at home. Although her parents were not wealthy, Edwina played the debutante at countless social functions, and she would later remember attending and giving elaborate parties wherever they went. She was a beautiful young lady, educated and eligible; still, although many eligible young men called at the Dakin home, at the age of 21 Edwina remained single—and a little concerned for her prospects, as many of her friends already were married and had children.

Cornelius Coffin Williams, Edwina's future husband, had come of entirely different stock. Thomas Lanier Williams II, Cornelius' father, was a Tennessee politician born in 1859 who had served as railroad commissioner for that state and as a commissioner for Mississippi at the 1893 World's Fair. He had run three gubernatorial campaigns, all of them unsuccessful, and his efforts to gain political influence by giving away considerable tracts of land nearly bankrupted his family. His wife died when their son Cornelius was only five years old, after which Cornelius was passed from aunt to aunt. As an adolescent, he was sent first to a seminary school, where he was extremely unhappy, and later to a military academy, where he conducted himself badly enough to spend a good deal of his time in the guardhouse. Openly hostile to authority, he was finally removed from boarding schools altogether; but this did not end his schooling, for he then spent two years at the University of Tennessee. On leaving the University, he enlisted in the U.S. Army in order to take part in the Spanish-American War (1898). It was his time in the military that first introduced him to heavy drinking and other forms of debauchery—including the all-night poker game, which would later result in a major alteration of his fortunes. One suspects he made an effort to collect himself when, in 1906, he was introduced to Edwina Dakin, the daughter of the local minister of Columbus, Mississippi.

At the time, Edwina was seeing a gentleman named Franklin Harris; Harris was not yet officially a suitor, but his calls had become noticeably frequent. In May of that year, Harris brought Cornelius Williams, a young visitor from Memphis, to the Dakin home; Harris assured the family that Cornelius was descended from one of the most elite families of Knoxville. With his considerable girth and military bearing, Cornelius cut an imposing figure. Edwina learned that he had served in the Spanish-American War as a second lieutenant; he was a handsome young man, even though a bout with typhoid fever during the war had claimed most of his hair. At the time, the telephone was the latest technological innovation, so the telephone industry was the perfect milieu for the up-and-coming—and Cornelius worked for the Cumberland Telephone and Telegraph Company, which added respectability to his personal charms. His lineage, too, was to be applauded; he came from the Williams, Coffin, Sevier, and Lanier families, each of which boasted a coat of arms and a rich history. All told, Cornelius Williams made a very acceptable suitor.

The early days of their courtship were punctuated by lapses in contact on his part, to such an extent that between May and August Edwina hardly heard from him. In mid-September, though, Edwina was stricken with typhoid fever and malaria, and during her illness Cornelius impressed her with thoughtfulness and attention, sending roses nearly every day and inquiring constantly about her health. Cornelius proposed to her on several occasions, and each time she turned him down. But he wasn't the kind of man who would take no for an answer—a trait that, as his wife, Edwina would later come to despise—and in time she gave in. (Edwina would never say that she had fallen in love with Williams' father, only that he had swept her off her feet.)

Cornelius had been promoted by this time to a managerial position over three telephone exchanges in Gulfport, Louisiana, so he had no trouble in convincing Reverend and Mrs. Dakin that he was worthy of their daughter's hand in marriage. A sizable wedding was planned, but in the midst of the planning Cornelius' father became gravely ill, and his illness required his son's full attention. Cornelius spent as much time in

Knoxville as his work would allow, with little or no time left for Edwina. She was about to give up all hope of ever being married when she received word that he was coming to Columbus with the ring. On June 3, 1907, the two were married by Edwina's father in a very small ceremony at St. Paul's Episcopal Church in Columbus. The couple moved to Gulfport, Mississippi, where they lived happily. Cornelius' job paid well, and the two were deeply involved in the social life of the small coastal town.

A year later, Thomas Lanier Williams died; Cornelius would never fully recover from the grief. His mourning followed the same pattern as the rest of his emotional life: he kept his immediate family in the dark, and most of what they ever learned of him came from Ella and Isabel, his father's two sisters.

In 1909, two events caused major change in the lives of the Williams family. The first was Cornelius' break with the telephone company, for reasons never made clear. He moved on to a position as a traveling salesman, which seems to have suited him well. The second event was Edwina's announcement that she was pregnant—to which Cornelius gave little or no response. Since her husband was away from home a great deal, Edwina decided to move from Gulfport back to Columbus in time for the birth. This arrangement was agreeable to all involved, especially Reverend and Mrs. Dakin, who were thrilled to have their only daughter in their home again. Cornelius retained his private life on the road, and Edwina once again began to enjoy social life in Columbus. Still, their relationship can't have been entirely distant, for Rose Isabel Williams was born at the rectory on November 19, 1909 and Thomas Lanier Williams III two years later. The boy who would become Tennessee Williams was born at a small hospital near the rectory on Sunday, March 26, 1911; Edwina would move into the rectory permanently, with the children, soon thereafter.

Little Rose was jealous of the new baby in the early years. "Let's shoo him away, Grandfads," she would say to her grandfather Dakin; "Grandfads" became her pet name for their grandfather, though all three of the Williams children referred to their grandmother Dakin simply as "Grand." Thomas, on the other hand, always adored his older sister, and he followed her everywhere. Her initial jealousy was soon overcome, and the two became inseparable. Both children were blue-eyed, their heads covered with blond ringlets, and they were often mistaken for twins. In the absence of their father, the two children came under the influence of their loving mother and grandparents, who read to them as often as possible. The minister's vast library became an object of wonderment. Thomas, who would become Tennessee Williams, remembers his grandfather quoting lines of poetry from memory—and he remembers finding those quotations fascinating.

The beginning of Williams' love of storytelling seems to date to this period; indeed, it is at this point that another storyteller, perhaps the principal storyteller of his childhood, entered the picture. Williams' nurse, Ozzie, was an African-American woman who had just appeared on the doorstep in rags one day, asking for work. Edwina had clothed and fed the girl and employed her at a decent wage, and she would later teach Ozzie to read and write. Ozzie was a spinner of tales, and the children loved her for it. Although the Dakins felt that people of color were racially inferior and should "remember their place"—the attitude was not then uncommon—they were kind to Ozzie and treated her as family. As a young man, Williams described Ozzie as a source of wonderment that rivaled his father's library:

> [I]n the evenings, when the white moonlight streamed over our bed, before we were asleep, our Negro nurse Ozzie, as warm and black as a moonless Mississippi night, would lean above our bed, telling in a low, rich voice her amazing tales about foxes and bears and rabbits and wolves that behaved like human beings.

Days at the rectory for Thomas were tranquil—that is, until Cornelius appeared. "Often the voice of my father was jovial or boisterous," he would later recall. "But sometimes it was harsh. And sometimes it sounded like thunder. To a small boy, he looked awfully big. And it was not a benign bigness. You wanted to shrink away from it, hide yourself."

The influences of his father and of his grandfather, both powerful, contrasted sharply. Walter Dakin's constant preaching, along with the gentler influence of both his mother and his other grandparents, fostered a strong Christian conscience. This was in conflict with the wilder, more cavalier disposition of the Williams family, and Thomas found the tension between the extremes of character difficult to manage.

The contradictions of his childhood would inform both his work and the rest of his life.

In 1914, the family moved to Nashville, the town in which Williams would later remember feeling the greatest happiness of his childhood. Nashville was a large city, and while the family lived there the adults were kept busier than ever with church business, leaving Rose and Thomas in Ozzie's care more often, and for longer periods of time, than they had done before. When Thomas began his first day of kindergarten, at the age of four, he was enchanted by the room and all the toys; but as soon as his mother left, he wailed for her so loudly that Edwina could hear him from half a block away. She quickly returned and took him home.

In the following year, the family moved to Clarksdale, Mississippi, where once again Reverend Dakin resurrected a dying church. Clarksdale was a rural town, much smaller than Nashville and much less sophisticated than Columbus. It was here that Williams experienced a traumatic event that would change his life forever: in the summer of 1916, he became gravely ill with diphtheria. Death in childhood from diphtheria was not uncommon at the time, and Thomas' illness was severe enough to cause concern; but Edwina's vigilant care—for nine nights she slept by his side, applying ice to his throat to prevent his choking to death—saved her son's life. Still, the bout with diphtheria left Williams with a terrible fear of suffocation. As he recovered, the boy found that he was unable to walk, so he pushed himself about on a miniature car called an "Irish mail" until he regained his mobility. He also learned how to play quiet, solitary games during his convalescence. He'd been a bully before, but now he was much more contemplative. "I was becoming a decided hybrid, different from the family line of frontiersmen-heroes of east Tennessee."

Having very nearly lost him, Edwina became very protective of her son. Cornelius claimed she was turning him into a "sissy" and resented the attention she paid to Thomas, who throughout his life would show symptoms of anxiety and hypochondria. Shortly after his illness, Ozzie disappeared. She was in the habit of working in the cotton fields every summer, so her yearly departure was to be expected, but one fall, for the first time, she failed to return. Although he was told that her leaving was not his fault, the incident tormented him, for not long before her disappearance he had called her "a big black nigger." Williams would feel a tremendous guilt over this for years.

In 1917, the United States entered the war that had escalated in Europe, World War I. By the hundreds, young men were enlisting to join the fighting forces overseas. As a result, many companies were severely shorthanded, and the International Shoe Company, where Williams' father worked, was no exception. Cornelius, exempt from service because of poor eyesight, was asked to fill a managerial position in St. Louis. He accepted the job, and this meant that he would have to move his family from the rectory to a new home in St. Louis. The move would turn Thomas' world upside down.

St. Louis

Cornelius Williams traveled to St. Louis ahead of his family, not to find a residence for them, but rather to begin his new job. Meanwhile, on a sweltering July day in 1918, Edwina and her seven-year-old son arrived in St. Louis by train. (It had been decided that young Rose would remain at home with the Dakins, but Edwina would not go anywhere without her Tommy, so mother and son had traveled to St Louis together.) Cornelius was on hand to meet them and led them out of the station, and to Thomas the crowds were overwhelming. As they left, Thomas reached out to pick a grape from a fruit stand and was startled by a sharp slap. His father's voice thundered, "Never let me catch you stealing again!" Confused that his father would assume his intention had been to steal, Thomas was humiliated. The moment would remain lodged in his memory.

The Williams family settled into a boarding house, and shortly afterward Edwina developed a case of the mumps; the doctor informed her that she was also pregnant. Being pregnant and ill in the heat of a St. Louis summer before the days of air conditioning was almost unbearable, but still Edwina ventured into the city in search of a home for her family. She hated St. Louis from the outset, and every negative incident that occurred heightened this as she retreated into memories of the happier times of her youth. She related anecdotes from these days to Thomas until he knew by heart every incident of her early days. After much searching, Edwina located a six-room apartment at 4633 Westminster, situated at the edge of an exclusive district. The house was spacious and had a somewhat Southern look—both points in its favor—

but the Williams apartment faced north, allowing very little light to enter its rooms. After the well-lit, expansive rooms of the rectory, this place seemed dreary at best; but it was better than the boarding house.

Cornelius Williams now felt stifled and uncomfortable at his desk job. The transition from independent, successful traveling salesman to respectable St. Louis businessman with a family to care for was nearly impossible for him, as Edwina recalled: "He was a very restless man.... He would always want to be out doing something." That fall, Williams and his sister were enrolled at the Eugene Field Elementary School. Williams thought it looked like a prison, but in fact he found it *worse* than a prison. He endured the teasing not only from the other children there, but from teachers as well. They mocked him for being the newcomer, for his Southern accent, for his diminutive stature, and for his reluctance to play the rough-and-tumble games expected of boys. He would admit later how terrified he had been of everyone:

> I can remember gangs of kids following me home yelling 'Sissy!'—and home was not a very pleasant refuge. If I had been born to this situation, I might not have resented it so deeply. But it was forced upon my consciousness at the most sensitive age of childhood.

The snobbery of the people in St. Louis was perplexing to the Williams family. In the South prominence was lineage or social standing; it was considered improper or uncouth even to mention a relationship between wealth and reputation. Williams' mother struggled to overcome this by aligning herself as best she could with the upper crust of St. Louis society. This was particularly difficult because Cornelius withheld money as a means of controlling his wife. Although small in size, Edwina stood up to her overbearing husband, berating him for his drinking and long poker nights. He in turn upbraided *her* for spoiling the children and not disciplining them properly. The bickering between them was constant. Williams was often a target of his father's anger and frustration with his wife. He often called his son a "sissy"; he is known to have said of his son, "Here comes Miss Nancy." These comments confused Williams, who all the while sought his father's love and approval desperately. As he saw no way to bridge the widening gap between them, he grew adept at withdrawing into his own imagination. For his sister Rose, on the other hand, there was no such escape.

In February of their first year in St. Louis, Williams' mother gave birth to a second son, Walter Dakin Williams. (He was named after his grandfather; to avoid the confusion of two Walters, he was simply called Dakin.) At first, Williams' father resented having another mouth to feed, but later he would use Dakin as another weapon against Williams, his sister Rose, and their mother, by showing preference to Dakin by granting him undue favors. In the spring of 1920, Williams' mother grew unwell from the mounting stress of life in the home, and her own mother agreed to take the train to St. Louis to help with the housework for a while. It was also decided that Williams should go to Clarksdale and spend some time at the rectory. During this three-month visit, Williams and his grandfather formed a bond even greater than they had enjoyed before. In the peaceful setting of Clarksdale, Williams excelled at his schoolwork—to such a degree that he advanced from the second to the fourth grade in one school year. Upon his return home, though, he grew to hate St. Louis more than ever, and this hatred extended to his father.

The end of World War I ushered in an almost total breakdown of the social systems of the nineteenth century—the Jazz Age. The young conducted themselves in ways that their parents and grandparents would never have dreamed of. Technological innovations, such as the radio and the automobile, were causing momentous changes in social standards. Williams' sister, Rose, once an active and curious young girl eager to win her father's love, became more and more rebellious. She was unable to be the musician her mother wanted her to be, and one attempt at acting (in a school play) nearly devastated her. She seemed to excel at nothing. Her behavior baffled their mother, who now felt alienated from her husband *and* her daughter. Williams and his sister had been close allies throughout their youth, but Rose's adolescent interest in boys left Williams, who did not understand his sister's physical and emotional changes, feeling rejected and extremely lonely. In all, the Williams family would relocate nine times while in St. Louis, and Edwina used each relocation as an opportunity to improve the family's social standing. One such relocation was initiated in order to place Rose in the affluent Soldan High School and Williams in Blewett Junior High School.

Rose dropped out of school after the first quarter, whereupon her mother and grandmother scraped together enough money to enroll her at Hosmer Hall, a private school for girls. After this second plan failed,

Rose was eventually sent to an Episcopal school for girls in Vicksburg, Mississippi—a school of the type that Edwina Williams had attended as a girl—for Edwina was convinced that the discipline at this school would resolve her daughter's rebelliousness. This separation from his sister further isolated Edwina's son, who was already solitary. Edwina noticed that he had begun writing more and more, so she purchased a secondhand typewriter—and from the moment he received the device he never stopped typing. At first he used the "hunt and peck" system, but after a typing course he became a speed typist, a skill that would serve him well throughout his life. Yet the more his mother encouraged his writing, the more his father derided his efforts. In Cornelius' mind, writing—especially poetry—was foolishness and the *last* thing he wanted his son to be doing. Had it not been for the biweekly school newspaper, The *Junior Life*, Williams might have been totally lost in the mammoth school setting. His first published piece in this paper, a work entitled "Isolated," appeared on November 7, 1924. Also during this period, he entered every type of writing contest imaginable, and won several of them.

When Williams was eleven, he met Hazel Kramer, a girl from his neighborhood. Two years older than she, he was able to form a comfortable relationship with her that would last for many years. His friendship with Hazel, and his increasing confidence in his own writing, helped him to endure the years of turmoil at home and at school. At the same time, however, Williams began to develop phobias, such as claustrophobia and fears of death and of suffocation. He was handicapped further by an intense shyness that left him unable to look others in the eye without blushing. His inability to control this neurosis further humiliated him.

During Williams' years in high school, his mother was ill much of the time and underwent many surgical operations. The volatile atmosphere in the home had adversely affected him, too, both mentally and physically. Rose, away in Vicksburg, was not told the serious nature of Edwina's various maladies—which explains her light, newsy letters to home. For her own part, Rose did not reveal how miserable she was at the school, where there were no young men to speak of and very little fun was to be had outside the confines of the campus. With Rose away and Thomas busy with school and his typewriter, Cornelius Williams lavished his attention on Dakin, taking the younger boy to baseball games and even allowing him to sit in on a poker game he frequented. Dakin was growing tall; he had become almost a mirror image of his father, and the two seemed inseparable. In the summer of 1926, Williams' mother moved the family yet again, in order to place her son in University City High School, University City being just outside the St. Louis city limits. For ten miserable years the family lived in a crowded flat in a mustard-colored brick building there, at 6554 Enright Avenue. (This dismal place would later inspire the setting for *The Glass Menagerie*.)

Rose was often invited to visit relatives in Knoxville, Tennessee, where her Aunt Isabel was an undisputed member of the highest social echelon—but her visits may not always have been pleasant ones. Once, when Rose returned home more reticent than before, Williams assumed she'd had a lovers' quarrel. When he asked her about it, she said, "Aunt Ella and Aunt Belle only like charming people, and I'm not charming." Rose began to experience severe stomach pains at this time, as Williams puts it, "[a] shadow had fallen over her that was to deepen steadily through the next four or five years." The fighting in the Williams household expanded to include Rose again, and she fought bitterly with her father, after which she would flee, crying hysterically. When Edwina attempted to take her daughter's side, Cornelius would order the two of them out of the house. Thomas longed to escape his home, and his wish was granted when his grandfather Dakin invited him to tour Europe. The few days they spent in New York before embarking for Europe were devoted to sightseeing. They stayed in the Biltmore Hotel, dined at the Westchester Biltmore Club, and attended a Broadway play. It was the most time Williams had spent alone with Grandfads since his visit to the rectory at the age of nine. Rose remained at home.

While in Paris, Williams had a phobic reaction that terrified him so severely that he thought was going mad. While walking down a street alone, he began to contemplate the complexity of the human thought processes. As though to outpace the idea, he began to walk faster, and by the time he reached the hotel he was drenched with sweat. He told no one of the experience. The anxiety came again while he was in Cologne visiting a cathedral. The panic was so overwhelming that when the others had left he knelt to pray. When he did, he felt a hand placed upon his head—and, as he described it, "the phobia was lifted away as lightly as a snowflake." He had no doubt that it was the hand of "our Lord

Jesus," who he believed had touched him and driven out the madness. His thoughts turned to his friend Hazel; from Paris, he wrote her a note and signed it in French, "I am yours, with a heart full of love."

Williams returned to University City to find a check for $35 waiting for him, for a story accepted by the magazine *Weird Tales*. He was now a paid writer, published in a professional magazine. During his last year at University City High School, he joined the staff of *Pep*, the school newspaper. He wrote a series of travel features taken from the diary he had kept during his trip to Europe. It began to look as though Williams might be able to support himself as a magazine or newspaper writer, but he still longed to be a poet. In the spring, when Williams was scheduled to graduate, he misinformed his mother as to the time of the ceremony; she arrived in the afternoon of June 13, 1929 and soon was irate to learn that the ceremony had taken place in the morning. Williams, meanwhile, cared little for the ceremony or the diploma and was sequestered at the downtown library. This indifference to ceremonies and awards would be constant throughout his life.

After his graduation, there was discussion in the Williams household over where to send their son to college. Washington University was nearby in St. Louis, but Williams chose to attend the University of Missouri in Columbia; he and Hazel planned to attend the same college, with her going in the following year. But just before it was time to leave for the fall semester, his father, knowing that the Dakin side of the family could be counted on to take over, suddenly decided he did not want to foot the tuition bill. And he was right; whenever the family called for help, it was his mother-in-law Dakin who came to the rescue. (Williams would later comment that he had no idea how she could have spared the money, unless she'd been embezzling church funds.)

Conflicting stories abound in the Williams family about Cornelius' ploys to keep his son and Hazel apart. Edwina was certain that her husband had pressured Hazel's grandfather, who also worked at the International Shoe Company, to send Hazel to another college. Biographer Lyle Leverich contends that Hazel's grandfather sided with Cornelius, not wanting his granddaughter to marry Thomas Williams. Whatever the case, Hazel's plan to follow Williams to "Ol' Mizzou" was thwarted, and Williams left for college alone.

WILLIAMS AT OL' MIZZOU

The University of Missouri lay halfway between St. Louis and Kansas City. The small town of Columbia had grown up around the university and, coincidentally, was the home of the Hamilton-Brown Shoe Company—Cornelius' main competitor. The university was renowned for its school of journalism, which Williams planned to enter by his third year. He'd become convinced, through his father's insistence, that working for a newspaper was the only way to earn money writing. Edwina rode the Cannonball Express with him to help find a suitable boarding house in Columbia, and to ensure that her son was settled properly. Meanwhile, back home, his father was pulling strings to get his son into a fraternity. Since Cornelius had been in a fraternity, he believed it fitting that Williams do the same, so Cornelius contacted two cousins who had attended the University of Tennessee and were affiliated with the fraternity Alpha Tau Omega (ATO). The cousins in turn contacted their fraternity brothers in Columbia, who sent a delegation to the boarding house to convey a surprised young Williams to their quarters.

In retrospect, his becoming a part of ATO was a blessing. His shyness was becoming a problem, and belonging to a group gave him the sense of importance that he needed desperately at the time. An article about him appeared in the local newspaper, under the headline "Shy Freshman Writes Romantic Love Tales for Many Magazines." The headline and some of the facts were exaggerations, but the article's description of him was accurate: "He is little more than five feet tall. He has clean-cut features and smooth brown hair. His eyes, which have a look that seems thousands of miles away, add to the unapproachable and reserved appearance which he presents."

Soon after his arrival at school, Williams wrote to Hazel to propose marriage. She replied that they were too young to consider such a thing. (In fact—unbeknownst to her shy suitor—she was already interested in another young man.) It was also during his freshman year that Williams wrote his first serious play and became the first freshman to win an honorable mention in the Dramatic Arts Club One-Act Play Contest. All his early work was signed Thomas Lanier Williams. When he came home from school for the summer, he found a job as a door-to-door magazine salesman, teaming up with a young man from Tulsa, Oklahoma. He headed back to Columbia in the fall with great determination and applied himself to his studies.

In general, Williams' first year of college went well. While his fraternity brothers thought of him as odd, he did make friends and become involved in the usual social events. He and his roommate, Smitty, often double-dated. Aside from one short involvement with wrestling, Williams shunned sports, and he detested his training for the Reserve Officer Training Corps (ROTC). He was an accomplished dancer and a sought-after partner. He was known particularly for his strange laugh—he called it his "mad cackle"—which would burst out with a strangled sound at inopportune times. It was endearing to some and frustrating to others, and it earned him a reputation as the dimwit of the frat house.

During Williams' second summer home, his father put him to work in the typing pool at one of the divisions of the International Shoe Company (where, incidentally, he would work with a young man named Stanley Kowalski). Life at home that summer was almost unbearable, for the quarreling was nonstop. At one point Cornelius slapped his sister Rose across the face, sending her screaming from the house. His father was continuing to withhold needed funds from his family, pointing to the faltering Depression economy as his excuse. But he continued to enjoy his golf, weekend poker games, and country-club membership. By now, he was spending entire nights away from the house, giving to Edwina no indication of his whereabouts. In the fall of his third year, Thomas came home for Thanksgiving; this sojourn included the worst fight yet, after which Cornelius actually packed his bag and left. (Rose wept all that night, certain that the family would end up in the poorhouse.) Williams delayed his return to school, not wanting to leave his mother and siblings in such a disrupted state. Part of him wanted to free his mother from this situation, and another part of him wanted to run away and pretend that none of it was happening. The strain of it all intensified his already considerable inner discord.

Williams' first taste of the University's journalism program was not pleasant. He hated reporting on dull things—obituaries or the prices of commodities. In order to spend more time on the writing he loved, he neglected his studies. At the same time, a girl named Anna Jean had captured his attention. One of the poems he wrote to her was published in the 1932 college yearbook. The biggest disappointment of the year was when his play took only thirteenth place in the Dramatic Arts Club Contest; had his play won, it would have been produced by the drama school. The loss was hard on Williams, and several years would pass before he would attempt another play. He was ejected from the ROTC, but he didn't mind that, for in just one more year his schooling would be over and he would finally be out on his own. Cornelius, however, took the ROTC failure far more seriously. He felt that the ROTC had tried to "make a man out of" his son, whom he often criticized for effeminacy, and he considered it evident that his son's failure had been deliberate. Furious, Cornelius pulled his son out of journalism school and employed him at the shoe factory—dusting samples, typing orders, and hauling around cases filled with sample shoes.

BACK AT HOME IN ST. LOUIS

Williams may well have wished to leave home and find other employment, but the timing was not right for such an undertaking; the Depression had left thousands out of work, and some were actually starving. In spite of the fact that he called it "a job designed for insanity" and "a living death," Williams had no choice but to resign himself. He at least had a job, and the little money he earned was his to keep. He bought his mother a print of the Mona Lisa, which she kept but never cared for, and then purchased an old car, for $29, whose sounds of operation earned it the nickname "Scatterbolt."

Each night, Williams retired to his attic room with his cigarettes, black coffee, and typewriter and wrote until he could write no longer. Often he would write all night long. He had stopped dreaming of ever making a living from his writing; he wrote because he knew no other means of expressing his thoughts on his situation. Away from school and his fraternity brothers, he was once again a loner. He had acquaintances among the employees at work, but they were not social companions. His regimen on the weekends was to spend Saturday afternoon at the downtown library reading, buying a 35-cent lunch at a restaurant, and then returning home to work on his story of the week, which he attempted to finish on Sunday afternoon. He spent the rest of the week mostly on poetry. In January of 1935, he won a competition hosted by the St. Louis Writers Guild for a story entitled "Stella for Star," and received $10. But on the heels of the good news came the bad: Williams learned a month later that Hazel Kramer had been married, to a man named Terry McCabe. Although six years had passed since his proposal, he still loved her deeply, and he was shaken.

Meanwhile, his sister Rose faced one life shattering experience after another, all unknown to her family, leading her to a total collapse. Her mind became too fragile for her to pursue employment, and every attempt was a dismal failure. Cornelius berated her constantly for not adding to the family's income. She and Thomas often attended movies and dances together, but even he could become impatient with her overreactions.

The definitive end to Rose's stability came as the two were coming home one night from a movie, in what was known as a "service car." Williams became increasingly tense, and he gradually lost the feeling in his hands and developed difficulty in breathing. As the car passed a hospital, he told the driver to pull into the emergency entrance; he was admitted, and upon examination it was found he was suffering from exhaustion and needed complete rest. Rose was calm at the hospital, but once she'd arrived home she lost control, running from room to room crying that they were all about to be murdered. Edwina would later recall, "It was as though Thomas' slight breakdown had destroyed the slender thread by which she had been hanging on to a reality she could no longer grasp."

Williams was kept in the hospital for a week, and on his return home he found Rose behaving more oddly than ever. One evening, she entered his bedroom and announced a plan: "Let's all die together." And while Rose was causing much worry, Cornelius expressed, perhaps for the first time, sincere concern for his elder son. The doctor assured them that Williams only needed rest, so it was decided that he would spend the summer in Memphis, where his grandparents had moved after Reverend Dakin's retirement. With great joy, Williams submitted his resignation from the shoe company, after which he received a letter from the company commending him on his "sterling qualities." Williams looked forward to this time out of his father's grip. While Cornelius berated Edwina for her possessiveness over Thomas, in truth it was Cornelius himself who held the greater sway. According to Williams, he always entered the house "as though ... with the intention of tearing it down from the inside."

The sojourn in Memphis turned out to be more than just a rest for Williams; it provided a proving ground for his work. There he met a neighbor of his grandparents, Bernice Dorothy Shapiro, who was a member of a little local theater. He wrote a play for the group entitled

Cairo! Shanghai! Bombay!, to which Shapiro wrote the prologue and the epilogue, for production by her theater group. Williams enjoyed watching the production and listening to the audience's response—laughter in all the right places and then the warm applause—and he returned to St. Louis convinced that playwriting would be his career. He found the family in better spirits than he expected; Edwina had at last convinced Cornelius to purchase a house, a quiet and spacious colonial home close to Washington University, and for a time the move from the crowded apartment seemed to calm the family's tensions. Both parents were now seriously concerned over the health of their two high-strung children. No one made any suggestion that Williams should resume his position at the shoe factory.

When the Webster Groves Theatre Guild announced a one-act play contest in the spring of 1936, Williams quickly wrote a play and entered. His play, The *Magic Tower*, was chosen for production. On opening night, three plays were performed, with judges on hand to decide the winner. At the close, the winner was announced as Howard Williams, but this person could not be found; the name was erroneous, but Williams, seated in the audience with his mother, Rose, and Dakin, was too shy to speak up. He was finally pushed to the front, where he won a silver plate—although he had hoped that the prize would be in cash.

Williams began to take night classes at Washington University in the hope of gaining enough credits to become a senior and eventually earn an undergraduate degree. There he met Clark Mills McBurney, a poet who would later drop his last name and write as Clark Mills. The two became a "literary factory," as they called it, in McBurney's basement, where they would spend hours writing. Mills introduced Williams to poets he referred to as the "purer voices in poetry"; one of these was Hart Crane, whose work fascinated Williams. In his journals during this time, Williams notes that he swam every morning, a practice that he would continue throughout his life, no matter where he was in the world.

In St. Louis, Williams became associated with a local theater group called the Mummers, a small, impoverished company doing everything within its power just to stay afloat. He wrote for them a quick play called *Headlines*, which they produced, neglecting to put Williams' name on the program. He seems not to have minded, though, for he went on to work with them on two of his full-length plays, *Candles to the Sun* and *The Fugitive Kind*. The former, a drama about coal miners, was particularly well received, and Williams was written up in the St. Louis newspapers.

The calm in the Williams household had been temporary. Rose became interested in a bachelor, Roger Moore, who lived across the street from their new home. He was running for mayor of University City, and Williams and Dakin helped to hand out campaign literature. Roger and Rose began spending a lot of time together, and the relationship appears to have become profound and serious. But Roger lost the election, after which he suffered a nervous breakdown and was taken to a private sanitarium; while there, running from the attendants, he was killed by a passing truck. His death buffeted Rose's already precarious mind.

At this time, the dynamic of the Williams family began to shift, and Cornelius' position to weaken. Despite a few scandals, his job had been secure through the Depression years, and this security had given him strength. But now a fight broke out at one of his Saturday night poker games, and in the melee Cornelius' ear was bitten off. Plastic surgeons grafted skin from his buttocks to reconstruct the ear, and the humiliation of this was a major strain.

While he recovered at home, Cornelius pressured Rose to find employment again, and she did, as a receptionist in a dentist's office. This job lasted only one day, for she became overwhelmed by the business of the office and locked herself in the bathroom, and her mother had to be called to come and talk her into unlocking the door. This was Rose's last attempt at employment.

After this came a confrontation between Williams and Rose that Williams would regret for the rest of his life. One evening in their parents' absence, Williams hosted a party which grew wild. Rose, upstairs listening, heard some of the guests making obscene telephone calls. She reported this to her mother, who demanded furiously that Williams never again invite his friends to their house. Williams' anger flared at Rose, and he yelled, "I hate the sight of your ugly old face!" Like his ill-advised words to Ozzie many years before, he could not take these back. Rose was stunned. Following this incident his anxiety came back worse than ever as he watched Rose sink into insanity. She was taken to see one doctor after another, but it was all in vain. Rose's condition seemed to improve when she visited her aunts in Knoxville, but when she returned home it always grew worse. Her hatred for her father was overt, and the doctors warned that Rose might try to take his life. She was committed to a mental hospital, and the family was told that insulin-shock therapy—a treatment, then very new in the United States, in which sufficient insulin was introduced into the bloodstream to cause seizure and thereby reduce symptoms of schizophrenia, mania, or depression—was the only hope. Edwina Williams agreed to the treatment; soon, visitors could hear Rose screaming like a wild animal as they approached her room.

Cornelius didn't know that his son was enrolled for classes in fall semester at the University of Iowa; indeed, he was unaware even that Williams intended to return to college. Once there, Williams would become part of the University's theater department, headed by Professor Edward Charles Mabie. It offered theatrical workshops, where projects were being produced continually, and a full-size theater that included a revolving stage 36 feet in diameter. In order to be part of this school, Williams first had to be accepted; in letters home he made this seem an easy feat, but even though his writer friends in St. Louis wrote letters of recommendation, really he experienced many days of intense concern. He was accepted, on probation because of his poor showing at Washington University.

Williams had longed to be free of his family for some time and was eager to board the train bound for Iowa City. In a letter to Clark Mills, which, like much of his correspondence, he never sent, he wrote, "I feel such a prodigious excitement—in spite of a double sedative—that I must communicate my feelings to someone or else blow up.... But of course the important thing is that I am actually going. I never really believed in its possibility until I got on the train." In one last entry in his journal before his departure, he wrote, "No I haven't forgotten poor Rose—I beg whatever power there is to save her and spare her from suffering."

WILLIAMS IN IOWA

His time away from home did not turn out to be filled with the carefree days he'd dreamed of. His shyness and loneliness followed him to Iowa, as his journal entries indicate ongoing anxiety, constant tension, and heart palpitations. He even went so far as to call himself homesick; although on the surface he disliked dependency, he nonetheless would depend on the assistance of his mother and grandmother for many years to come.

Mabie proved to be a taskmaster, requiring all his students to be involved in every aspect of a play's production. Williams produced enormous amounts of work while in Iowa, maintaining the discipline he'd developed at home. In addition to writing and attending classes, he earned extra money by waiting tables at the cafeteria of the University's hospital. At first he refused offers of the ATO chapter to live at the fraternity house, for it was too far from campus; but he took the chapter up on its offer when it offered a lower rent, and once in his new residence he enjoyed the food, his room, and the camaraderie. It was at the University of Iowa that Williams first decided to use the pseudonym "Tennessee," for which choice he would give various reasons in later years. Among the more romantic of his accounts is this, given in Edwina Williams' *Remember Me to Tom*:

> ... Thomas Lanier Williams ... is a nice enough name, perhaps a little too nice. It sounds like it might belong to the sort of writer who turns out sonnet sequences to Spring.... Under that name I published a good deal of lyric poetry which was a bad imitation of Edna Millay. When I grew up I realized this poetry wasn't much good and I felt the name had been compromised, so I changed it to Tennessee Williams, the justification being mainly that the Williamses had fought the Indians for Tennessee and I had already discovered that the life of a young writer was going to be something similar to the defense of a stockade against a band of savages. (109)

He had to take summer classes to make up failed credits, but Williams finally received his bachelor's degree from the University in the late summer of 1938.

ROSE'S FINAL TRAGEDY; THE FRENCH QUARTER

No plan was in place to guide him after graduation. For a time he returned home to St. Louis, thinking his play *Not About Nightingales* would be produced by the Mummers; but the group had disbanded due to lack of funds. He then traveled to Chicago to join the Works Progress Administration Writers' Project—a federally subsidized project, in operation between 1936 and 1940, that supported local authors by employing them to record the oral history of pioneers—but was told his family's finances were too secure for him to qualify. Disappointed, he returned to St. Louis once again. After reading about a play contest sponsored by The Group Theater in New York, he packaged all his completed scripts and mailed them. He needed to be alone, to write something *new*, and he decided at last to try life in New Orleans.

New Orleans was proved to be a positive experience for Williams, and he would come to think of it as his favorite city in the world. Dressed in a conservative suit on arrival late in 1938, he looked like a tourist; but by New Year's Day of 1939 the bohemian life of the French Quarter began to relax his guarded nature. He found accommodation in a boarding house, at 722 Toulouse Street, and although he would soon find himself hungry and alone, still he would count his days there as some of the happiest of his life. The warm, mild climate and inexpensive food and lodging made the Quarter a center for all manner of artists, politicos, and malcontents—and Williams, considering himself among the greatest of these, felt right at home. He walked the streets for hours and enjoyed the Mardi Gras festivities, the museums, the arts, and the people. The scenes of voodoo cults, Creole people, open restaurants, Basin Street, and Dixieland jazz played over in his mind and would inform his later work. The social and sexual behaviors to which he was exposed there intensified his inner struggle between the Christian teachings of his grandparents and the attraction he felt toward members of his own sex. He began to think once again of moving on.

Accounts differ as to just when came the end to the violent phase of Rose's madness; it may have been while Williams was in Iowa, or during this time in New Orleans, or even as late as 1943, when he was in New York. She was living at St. Vincent's hospital, where her condition had continued to decline. Edwina Williams had lost much: like his brother, Dakin had moved out, and Cornelius—slipping into alcoholism—had totally given up on Rose, whose condition seemed hopeless. A new psychosurgical procedure was being touted as the answer for those confined to mental institutions, as Rose was: the prefrontal lobotomy. In this procedure—which would later be denounced as inhumane and of uncertain therapeutic value and abandoned by most institutions—the surgeon drilled a hole in each of the orbits of the skull and then severed the fibers that connect the frontal lobe to the prefrontal cortex and thalamus. A doctor at St. Vincent's recommended a prefrontal lobotomy for Rose, and Edwina, otherwise out of hope, consented to it. She would later admit that going ahead with the procedure had been a "grave mistake," that lobotomy "destroys something essential in a person's character." Dakin would say it had made Rose into a "mental vegetable." According to Edwina, too, after the operation Cornelius never visited his daughter again. Williams—in whichever phase of his life—was inconsolable. He would set aside a portion of his wealth in later days to ensure Rose's perpetual care.

CALIFORNIA: THE PARROTT ADVENTURE

When musician Jim Parrott moved into the Toulouse Street boarding house, Williams found a fast friend. The two were of about the same size, and both appeared deceptively young. (Williams was now nearing 30, but he still had to give proof of his age in bars.) The two scraped together their meager funds and lit out in Jim's Ford for the glitter and promise of California. Jim's uncle had offered them work on his pigeon ranch, so they even had a prospect of employment. Along the way, the adventurers saw destitute families walking beside the roads even in the desert areas; for most of his life Williams had been shielded from the losses of the Depression, but now he saw it all for himself. And money was short for him, too. When the duo had to choose between gas and food, they chose the food and siphoned gas from other cars to continue the trek. Letters that Williams sent home along the way helped his mother to know where to send the little she could sacrifice from her household account. The financial situation became so bad that Williams even appealed to his father for help; Cornelius told his son to contact a friend by the name of Sam Webb, who was connected with the shoe company. Williams did so.

Jim Parrott left him in Los Angeles, headed for his uncle's ranch. Williams took a room at a YMCA that faced Pershing Square, a small city park overflowing with homeless people, many of whom had set up camp there in desperation after a vain search for work. After a few days, a terrifying loneliness set in, and Williams telephoned Jim and joined him at the ranch. Jim's relatives treated Williams with gracious hospitality. He paid them room and board and helped on the ranch, killing and picking up squab and shoveling manure. Jim, meanwhile, found work at an airplane factory, which prompted Williams to comment in a letter that he believed America was truly gearing up for war.

Through Sam Webb, Williams secured a job working at Clark's Bootery, a shoe store in Culver City. He purchased a second-hand bicycle for the commute, and on every workday he passed the guarded gates of the MGM studios, hardly imagining that one day his name would be very important there. Williams seems to have been industrious—or at least, as his later behavior affirms, to have enjoyed the freedom of his bicycle. "Any boy who would ride a bicycle twenty-four miles a day to work," Webb wrote to Cornelius, "is bound to succeed."

Just a few days before his 29th birthday, Williams received word from New York that his group of one-act plays had won an award that would include a check for $100—a veritable godsend in the lean years of the Depression. The award came from the Group Theater, a group of renowned actors and playwrights that was known for establishing the fame of dramatic works—and whose name therefore carried considerable weight in New York. Once the check was safely in Williams' hands, his mother told all of St. Louis of her son's good fortune, but for the moment the playwright himself was just glad to be paid for his work. Williams did not yet realize that the Group award was a turning point in his career.

The prestige of the Group award also was the impetus for Cornelius Williams to produce one of the few letters he ever wrote to his son—opening with noncommittal talk about shoes but closing with "we were all very proud you won the $100 prize." The letter's signature is a testimony to the distance between father and son: "Affectionately, C.C. Williams."

Agents in New York, aware of the disposition of every major award, began contacting Williams. An offer from Audrey Wood, of the Liebling-Wood Agency, interested him the most; but even after her encouraging letter Williams hesitated, saying he'd like to think about her offer. Whereas many other aspiring playwrights might have taken Wood's hundred dollars and caught the next plane to New York, Williams instead bicycled down the coast to see Mexico, with Jim Parrot along for company. "Flights" of this kind would become a theme in his life whenever self-doubt plagued him, and in time Audrey Wood—with whom Williams' relationship was only beginning—would come to expect them.

Williams and Jim Parrott wiled away the days, living on the $100 prize, and correspondence was brisk between Williams and Wood. The honesty and sincerity of her letters gratified him; "... on the basis of what I have read," she once wrote, "... you are not a finished dramatist, although I do say I think you are highly promising." He accepted her as his agent, and the two would work together for thirty-two successful years.

Williams and Parrott ended up on a chicken farm near the beach at Laguna and enjoyed many carefree days there. Indeed, Williams seems to have experienced real rest and peace at the farm for the first time in recent memory: "It has been years since I have felt so calm and relaxed," he wrote in his journal. The humorous letters written to Wood, who was normally known to be "all business," charmed her, and she became a kind of mother to him—an effect Williams would have on other women in his life as well. At the same time, Wood was busily sending his work to prospective publishers, and eventually she received an acceptance from the prestigious *Story*. She also submitted his work for a grant from the Rockefeller Foundation. In California, Williams began to read the works of D.H. Lawrence. He recalled that Lawrence's widow lived in New Mexico, and he wrote to her; he received no reply, but his fascination with Lawrence was growing, and he began to think of adapting one of Lawrence's stories for the stage.

Parrot and Williams found each other's company less and less congenial, and they parted when Jim chose to move on to Pasadena.

WILLIAMS' CONSCIENCE CALLS HIM HOME

Low on funds, Williams implied in a letter to his mother that he might hitchhike back to St. Louis; the deception worked, and Cornelius sent money by way of Sam Webb. By now, Williams' conscience was troubling him for leaving his family for such a long period of time; but he dreaded going home and dallied wherever he could. He stopped off at Taos, New Mexico to locate Lawrence's widow, which he did, and through meeting Frieda Lawrence he became even more entranced with the author's legend.

Before beginning the second leg of his journey home, Williams wrote another letter, again hinting to his mother that funds were tight. She again sent him money, but still he hitchhiked from Denver.

No sooner had Williams arrived in St. Louis than he learned that Clark Mills, his poet friend from Washington University, meant to drive with another man to New York and that there was room in the car. Williams accepted their offer of a ride.

When Audrey Wood first met the retiring young man in her outer office, she thought him just another out-of-work actor. His small stature and shy demeanor were not at all reminiscent of the humorous letters or the photos—of a tanned young man on the beach at Laguna—that she had received from the Williams she knew. After the first awkward moments, though, she took a liking to the young playwright and showed him every possible favor, treating him to dinner and introducing him to influential people.

With war now raging in Europe and the United States claiming neutrality, the country's economy was in limbo. Other than jobs in munitions plants and airplane factories, employment was at a standstill. Even with the help of Wood and her friends, Williams couldn't find work. An entry in his journal reveals his desperation for a strong-willed mentor: "Met lots of people here but nobody does me much good. They're all so involved in their own lives. I need somebody to envelop me, embrace me, pull me by sheer force out of this neurotic shell of fear I've built around myself lately." Only one solution seemed feasible: returning home to his attic, where he could work without fear of destitution. This solution worked, but it was not ideal; "There is a kind of spiritual fungus or gangrene which sets in here after the second or third month's residence," he described it to Wood. "At the end of four you are pronounced incurable and committed to the wholesale shoe business for the rest of your life."

Under the miserable conditions back at home, waiting to see whether the Rockefeller grant would come through, Williams again wrote in the attic. At this point, the writing was his only hope, for nothing seemed to be going right. All his old friends in St. Louis were now happily married, with homes, cars, children, and mortgages. His mother was preparing for Christmas, a time of year that his father loathed. The cataracts Williams had contended with for several years were becoming ever more troublesome.

To make matters worse, his mother continually begged him to go with her to see Rose, a prospect he dreaded more than any other. But how could he refuse? During one visit Rose spouted ceaseless obscenities and laughed all the while. After the visit, Williams wrote in his journal, "It was a horrible ordeal. Especially since I fear that end for myself." But his mother awakened him on the very next morning with a telegram from Wood; he had received the Rockefeller grant, which would pay out $100 checks for 10 months and thus enable him to continue his work in New York City.

After spending the New Year in Memphis with his grandparents, Williams returned to New York, where he took a room at a YMCA for $7.50 a month. Now funded, he found himself immersed in the professional theater, meeting directors and actors, watching rehearsals during the day, and attending shows each evening. He also attended a seminar on advanced playwriting conducted at the New School for Social Research in Greenwich Village.

In February of 1940, his one-act play *The Long Goodbye* was produced by student actors at the New School, and the production was mentioned briefly in *The New York Times*. Williams was introduced to other struggling artists, several of whom—Donald Windham and Fred Melton initially, and then Gilbert Maxwell—would later join forces with him in various ways. Despite the joy of all this exposure, though, Williams felt the constant distractions of the city were keeping him from his writing; he redoubled his efforts, and soon his friends were amazed by his grueling work schedule. He could sit down at his typewriter anywhere and churn out manuscript pages at 90 words per minute, no matter what was going on around him. And his complete lack of attention to mundane details became notorious: laundry and half-eaten food filled the corners of his rooms, and although his friends warned him and gave him carbon paper repeatedly, he often sent out original manuscripts and then forgot where he'd sent them.

New Influences: Provincetown, Wood's Departure, and Mexico

By the spring of 1941, not much had improved in Williams' life. He felt himself becoming listless, overweight, and, worse, unproductive. To appease his characteristic need for a change of scenery, he planned a trip to Mexico; but before he could leave, word came that the Guild was interested in his *Battle of Angels*, so he had to stay close to New York. He told his mother that there might be a production of the play by the fall, and she wrote back with her own good news: his father had finally agreed to purchase a home. After all the years of shifting from apartments to rental houses, they were settling at 53 Arundel Place, still in St. Louis. The two-story house had an attic room that Edwina would prepare just for her playwright son, but Williams would feel no compulsion to occupy it soon.

For the summer, he needed a place to get away and write revisions of *Battle of Angels*. Wood suggested Provincetown, on Cape Cod, an idea that seemed as good as any other to Williams. ("In those days people were always putting me on trains or buses like I was a pawn in a chess game. Well, I must have wanted it that way. And that's the way I got it.") While in Provincetown, he began the first in a series of letters to Donald Windham—letters that Windham would later publish—that expressed shock at the homosexual lifestyle of Cape Cod, even as he was experiencing an intense inner struggle regarding his own sexuality. He continued to search for someone to love, who might love him in return, and during that summer he found that possibility. His prospect was a dancer known as Kip Kiernan—an expatriate Canadian whose real name was Bernard Dubowsky. Williams was drawn to the ruggedly handsome Kiernan, and they spent many long hours together through the summer months. Williams was frustrated with the slow progress of the *Battle* production, and Wood had moved to the West Coast, leaving Williams with feelings of abandonment; Kiernan helped him to work through all these feelings, and he became the focus of Williams' affection. But Kiernan had a girlfriend, whom he loved; as her distaste for Williams grew, Williams lashed out at her and thereby alienated Kiernan; eventually, the girlfriend turned Kiernan against him. "I'm always the fugitive," wrote Williams in his journal, "—will be till I make my final escape—out of life altogether."

In an effort to bolster his flagging spirits, Williams went to Mexico, where he stayed at the Hotel Costa Verde in Acapulco. The hotel offered hammocks, slung outside the screen doors, and a private beach bordered by a tropical rain forest. (The beach would become the setting for *The Night of the Iguana*.) Williams was astonished at the inertia and indifference of the people he saw there, caused, he believed, by relentless sunlight and strong drink. He also encountered bands of aggressive Nazis, who repulsed him so completely that he longed to have his own yacht to take him far away from all humanity. Still, there were worthy acquaintances to be formed there; it is in Acapulco that he met the writer Gordon Sager, as well as the writer and composer Paul Bowles and his wife, the writer (and committed lesbian) Jane Auer Bowles. Williams would become lifelong friends with Paul and Jane Bowles, and Paul would compose the musical scores to *The Glass Menagerie* in 1945 and *Sweet Bird of Youth* in 1959. Also while in Mexico, Williams read Carson McCullers' book *The Heart Is a Lonely Hunter*; he was so impressed by her writing that he thought his own work fraudulent by comparison.

BATTLE OF ANGELS FAILS PAINFULLY

On his way back to New York, he spent some time in the attic room his mother had prepared for him in their new house in St. Louis, awaited word of when rehearsals of his play would begin and when and where he would be needed. When the news came, Williams was drawn into a rush of events such as he had never experienced before—working with the directors, producers, actors, and stage technicians necessary to the production of a play—all of whom have ideas of how the production should be done. For a time there was even talk that Joan Crawford considered starring in the play, but only if she could make major changes to the script. That eventually fell by the wayside, but in general the magnitude of the experience was overwhelming.

Despite Boston's reputation for a conservative theatergoing audience—the play was somewhat risqué—it was decided that *Battle of Angels* would open there. But the choice was a poor one: on opening night, before the play's halfway mark, the audience was visibly upset, even ready to walk out. A catastrophe of stage effects sounded the play's death-knell: In rehearsal, a blowtorch that one scene required had not given off enough smoke, so someone had called for more, and the technical staff had provided it—so much, in fact, that the stage was lost in it and the audience sent choking and gasping to the exits.

This was Williams' first public failure. He told his mother in a letter that the audience had been non-poetic, but the truth wasn't quite that simple; when the company met on the following day to talk about resolving the play's problems, it became clear that the inexperienced playwright had little to contribute to the discussion. Rewrites were forthcoming, but the play would not be offered in New York at that time, and Williams would work on the script for many years. He struggled with the fear that no producer who had heard of the failure would take another chance on him; but even aside from Audrey Wood, he was surrounded by people who believed in his talent.

In January of 1942, Williams underwent the second of his four eye surgeries to correct his cataracts. During his recuperation he moved into an apartment shared by Don Windham, Fred Melton, Paul Bigelow, and Jordan Massee. As soon as he was sufficiently recovered, Williams traveled to Key West. A widow whom he met there, Mrs. Clara Black, ran a boarding house called The Trade Winds; she rented an elaborately appointed suite to him for $5 a night. He took to Key West immediately and mentioned wishing he were rich enough to stay on; and when Mrs. Black offered him the "slave quarters" in the back for only $8 a week, he took her up on the offer. Thus began Williams' love affair with Key West. Later he would spend much of his time in a home of his own there.

On the surface he seemed happy, but his journals reveal the fears and the loneliness that remained with him wherever he went. The failure of *Battle of Angels* was a great discouragement, and money was once again a constant issue. No matter how much he received, he spent it all and more, and he left a trail of debt wherever he went. Eventually, Audrey Wood was given power of attorney over his financial affairs, and she doled out money to him incrementally and kept the rest in a bank account for future need. Back in St. Louis, his mother had invited her parents to live with the Williams family in their spacious new house; but Cornelius now hated Reverend Dakin, so the tension in the home was worse than ever. On Williams' trip back to New York, he stopped off to see them, but he did not stay long.

A FEW YEARS WANDERING

The next few years of Williams' life became a hodgepodge of moves, traveling, writing, and taking on any menial job he could find. At one time, Williams worked as an elevator operator in a rundown hotel, and after that he worked as a uniformed usher in a movie theater for $17 a week. He was forced more than once to sell his possessions just to be able to eat. His horrific mood swings determined how well or how badly his writing progressed. Fascinated as he was with the writings of D.H. Lawrence, Williams decided to collaborate with Donald Windham on adapting one of Lawrence's stories for the stage. (The resulting play, *You Touched Me!*, would not see production for many years.)

In the fall of 1941, Williams was once again in New Orleans alone. There he received word that his grandmother was very ill. His mother sent him money to come home, but he did not want to go, even though his grandparents were the members of his family he loved the most. He went anyway.

On his way back to New Orleans, he heard the news of the bombing of Pearl Harbor; the United States would soon enter the war in earnest. Williams' poor eyesight earned him a classification of 4-F—ineligible for the draft due to physical shortcomings. (Dakin Williams *was* eligible, and he would soon be drafted into active service.)

Windham and Williams finished a draft of *You Touched Me!*, and Wood tried unsuccessfully to sell it. Williams headed south once again, this time finding work as a Teletype operator in St. Augustine, Florida at $120 a month. He worked nights; this left his mornings free for writing. During this time, he became acquainted with Margo Jones, a wealthy Texan who loved the theater; Jones had earned the nickname "the Texas Tornado" for her ability to "make things happen" in theaters across the country. In the spring of 1943, Williams had just turned 32 and had no obvious means of supporting himself, and thought himself a failure. Just when everything looked the bleakest, though, he received a telegram from Wood telling him she found him a job as a scriptwriter for the major film studio MGM, offering $250 a week. Williams couldn't believe the proposed wage—"That's dishonest!" he said to Wood—but the opportunity was too good to pass up.

LIFE AT MGM

Williams traveled to California by train, a trip that lasted three days and two nights. As soon as he arrived, he found his way to the MGM studios. When Williams was first hired, he was told that he would be rewriting a novel into a screenplay for Clark Gable; however, he soon learned the project had been shelved until Gable returned from service in the war.

He further learned that writers in Hollywood were looked down upon by actors and directors. Nearly all the famous writers of the time, especially playwrights, were persuaded to work for the movies only by the lure of sizable paychecks.

Williams was embarrassed at the opulence of the office he was given on the second floor at MGM, and he knew that his lifestyle would never mesh with what was happening in Hollywood. His first assignment was to write a script for Lana Turner, and he was instructed to make it simple. Compared to the deeply moving work he'd been producing, the whole idea was ludicrous. "I feel," he wrote to Audrey Wood, "like an obstetrician required to successfully deliver a mastodon from a beaver." Back in New York, the "Texas Tornado," Margo Jones, finished reading *You Touched Me!* and liked it immensely—but more than the play, she was interested in the future of the playwright himself. Just as Wood was doing, she hovered over him with motherly affection; she made sure he had all the right clothes for the right occasions and built connections for him to "the right people." Williams loved this treatment and hated it; he liked it while it was happening but would always hate himself later for needing others so much. This resentment was beginning to build against Wood, for it was she who did the most for him. For years, he had turned to her for every detail of the management of his career.

Working on the Lana Turner script was one of the most difficult things Williams had ever had to do, for he'd never before had to write on assignment *for* anyone and he found the conditions difficult. He returned to his own work in the evenings, though, and eventually produced the story "The Gentleman Caller," which would provide the framework for the later *The Glass Menagerie*. The story, which he planned to write for both stage and screen, was based on the tragedy of his sister's life. He didn't believe Rose was truly schizophrenic, he wrote at the time, but that "the petals of her mind had simply closed through fear"; and as the glass figurines in the play represented the precarious balance of the main character's personality, so too did they symbolize the fragmentary nature of his sister's existence. His hope was to interest MGM in this work and in other pieces that he'd written on his own terms, rather than continue to write on assignment; but this wasn't to be. (Many critics agree, in retrospect, that had MGM accepted Williams' story as a movie the piece probably wouldn't have survived past its screenplay.)

Williams continued his assignments for the studio, but between assignments reported to his office ever less frequency, shutting himself up in his apartment instead to write for hours on end. This was the first time he'd ever been able to write while making money, and he made the most of the opportunity. Wood continued to collect his paychecks from the studio, depositing them in a New York bank and doling out to him $100 a week. Although the MGM work wasn't creatively fulfilling, the arrangement was at least financially comfortable.

The situation changed drastically, though, when Williams refused MGM's request to write something for the child star Margaret O'Brien. From that point on the studio "blackballed" him, that is, exerted all possible influence to deny him work. Other writers at the time were allowing their creative energies to be "channeled" by the Hollywood executives—which many called "selling out"—and thereby made a living, but Williams was seduced by neither profit nor prestige. Solitary and introspective, he focused more on the aesthetic concerns of his own work than on commercial credit; he explained to Wood in a letter, "Let's face it! I can only write for love." The studio did not renew his contract, of course, but he continued to receive paychecks for six months after his departure from Hollywood. In fact, MGM would regret the loss of Williams and the manuscript of *The Glass Menagerie*; Warner Brothers would later profit immensely from the film rights to both that play and *A Streetcar Named Desire*.

WILLIAMS AT HOME AGAIN

In Cleveland, Margo Jones had found a producer for *You Touched Me!*, the play based on the work of D.H. Lawrence; but the script had been changed so much that she didn't want Williams to see it. As this project evolved, Williams' relationship with Donald Windham became strained and Williams became less enthusiastic about sharing billing or royalties. While Williams was still in Hollywood, his father visited the coast on a business trip. Fearing that Cornelius would appear at his doorstep unannounced—and, presumably, learn something that Williams did not want him to learn—Williams kept his blinds drawn and the door locked. But Cornelius sent word for his son to meet him at his hotel, and there the two had the first private conversation they'd had in many years. Williams emerged from this conversation with a view of his father as a pitiful, lonely old man who, like his son, was desperate for love.

Some time after this meeting, Williams once again felt duty-bound to return home, which he planned to do on his way back to New York. First, though, he paid a visit to Frieda Lawrence in New Mexico to discuss *You Touched Me!*; he found that she was pleased by what he had written about her husband. Much was the same at home: Dakin was on leave from the service for Christmas, and their grandmother was still gravely ill. But this time Williams needed no money from his mother.

Although Williams' grandmother was quite frail, she helped busily with the housework in preparation for the holidays. On the evening of January 6, 1944, Williams left the house as his grandmother played something by Chopin on the piano; when he returned home, she was dying upstairs. The effect that her dying, and her death, had on him is hard to pinpoint—he had a proclivity for the morose—but he did not attend the funeral, and soon afterward he completed his return to New York.

THE GLASS MENAGERIE: WILLIAMS' FIRST MAJOR SUCCESS

He finished a rewrite of "The Gentleman Caller" there and then started a new play, 60 pages of which he wrote in only five days. (In his journals are several passages describing the numerous revisions this manuscript would undergo.) In March of 1944, he received an award of $1,000 from the National Institute of Arts and Letters for *Battle of Angels* and for a collection of his one-act plays. This award helped to restore his faith in *Angels*, which had been sorely tested at the play's Boston premiere. Williams spent that summer in Provincetown, where he began to transform "The Gentleman Caller" into *The Glass Menagerie*. He didn't think the play would have commercial appeal: "Of course I liked the material because it was so close to me," he wrote to Margo Jones, "but for that very reason I doubted that it would come across to others." Still, he gave the new play to Audrey Wood when he returned to New York— and she recognized it immediately as better than anything else he'd written. She searched for a producer the very next day and soon chose the multitalented Eddie Dowling, who by that time had been writing, composing, producing, directing, and performing for almost thirty years. Dowling liked the play but wasn't convinced it would make money; but he was nevertheless able to secure financial backing from Louis Singer.

In the spring of 1945, *Menagerie* surprised everyone by becoming an instant success in Chicago, and it was quickly moved back to New York. The success in Chicago almost ensured that New York audiences and critics would like the play, and like it they did: the reviewers praised the play's originality and dogged intensity. A telegram Williams sent to his mother at the time read: "Reviews all rave. Indicate smash hit. Line block long at box office. Love, Thomas." She received a parcel containing legal documents a few days later, and she learned that her son had signed over to her half of all the proceeds from *The Glass Menagerie*. Williams also made sure that his mother was present at the big party he threw in New York in late April of that year. His father did not want to attend, but his grandfather did; Williams lodged them in one of the finer hotels, and Reverend Dakin turned out to be the life of the party.

The play won many accolades at the time and was chosen for performance at the Franklin D. Roosevelt birthday celebration at the National Theater in Washington, D.C. Despite this success, though, Williams had doubts; he believed that a "yesterday's self" had created *Menagerie*, and he was unsure that he could now reproduce the circumstances that had made it possible. This dilemma led him back to Mexico, where he began work on *The Poker Night*, which would become *A Streetcar Named Desire*.

Even in Mexico, Williams could not quite escape New York. Telegrams arrived regarding the casting for *You Touched Me!*, which was scheduled to open in Boston in the following fall. By this time, the script bore little resemblance to the original. Williams traveled back to New York and arrived in time for the opening; the play earned uninspiring reviews, and its reception was no less discouraging to Williams than his experience in Boston had been.

The producers decided to move *You Touched Me!* to the Booth Theater in New York—even as *The Glass Menagerie* continued to play in town—and the play opened there on September 26, 1945. The reception was tepid from the very beginning, and the production closed on January 5, 1946; the playwright would never again see this work performed in a major venue. Williams saw his collaboration with Windham as a failure, and he decided to work with only his own material from that point on. In welcome contrast to *You Touched Me!*,

Menagerie ran for an entire year, despite the feud between Dowling and Taylor, which had reached its boiling point. (Laurette Taylor would die a few months after *Menagerie's* close, and Williams would venerate her, in an emotional article for *The New York Times*, as one of the few performers he'd that he ever met who could truly embody his characters.)

After *You Touched Me!* closed, Williams spent time in New Orleans writing a draft of the play *Ten Blocks on the Camino Real*; he submitted the manuscript to Audrey Wood, who told him to hide it forever. Depressed and discouraged, he bought an old Packard and decided to drive back to Taos, New Mexico to see Frieda Lawrence. He stopped in St. Louis on the way. His brother, Dakin, had recently returned from the war and was living at home. Cornelius had retired and now spent most of his time drunk and/or skulking around the house. Reverend Dakin, terrified of Cornelius, seldom ventured from his bedroom upstairs. It was at this time that Dakin, Williams' younger brother, began to suspect that Williams might be homosexual. With a sister who'd gone insane and a father who was an alcoholic, this thought was more than he was willing to tolerate, so he went down to the Air Force recruiting office and reenlisted. "It was a lot rougher at home," he later recalled, "than slugging it out in the service during World War II."

Williams was soon to have another of his many close encounters with mortality. He experienced severe abdominal pain before leaving St. Louis for Taos, but his profound fear of death kept him from seeking help of any kind. The pain worsened on the road—and then the Packard broke down. Williams spent a few days in a hospital in Wichita, Kansas, where he was told that he had appendicitis that was not yet acute; by the time he reached Taos, he was convinced he was dying. He wrote a will at a local hospital before the necessary surgery, and as he went under the ether he vociferously announced to all that he was dying. He recovered a few days later.

Williams spent the summer of 1946 in Nantucket, inviting Carson McCullers to join him because he so admired her work. He suggested that McCullers make a play out of her book *Member of the Wedding*, and the idea appealed to her. The two worked together every morning at a long table set up in the front room of the cottage, Williams on his portable typewriter at one end of the table, and McCullers at the other. Their afternoons were spent swimming, and in the evenings McCullers played the old upright piano or they read each other poetry. In New York, casting took place for the road company for *The Glass Menagerie*, while Wood continued to negotiate for the movie rights. In the fall, Williams gave the play *Summer and Smoke* to Margo Jones, which she added to her production schedule for 1947. McCullers, on the other hand, had a difficult time finding a backer for her own play—until Williams presented it to Wood. The play would be produced in 1949 and win the New York Drama Critics' Circle Award in the following year, but Williams would never take credit for this success or mention it much in any interview.

A STREETCAR NAMED DESIRE

As Wood read the script for *The Poker Night*, she knew her client had another hit. Williams and his grandfather were staying together in a hotel room in Key West when Wood requested that he meet her in Charleston to discuss the play with the producer Irene Mayer Selznick, the former wife of the director David O. Selznick and the daughter of the film mogul Louis B. Mayer of MGM. A deal was struck during this meeting, and Wood wired her New York office with satisfaction: "Blanche is coming to stay with us."

Williams originally wanted Elia Kazan to direct the play, now entitled *A Streetcar Named Desire*, but Kazan wasn't enthusiastic about the script. Luckily, Williams was a friend of Kazan's wife, Molly Day Thatcher, who was an important member of the Group Theatre. It was Thatcher who persuaded Kazan at last to take on the project. And it was lucky for Williams that she did; Kazan was prominent enough in the theater community to outnegotiate the inexperienced Irene Selznick, who was relatively new to the business. In the resulting contract, Kazan reduced Selznick's role in the production to that of an owner and thereby freed himself to work directly with the playwright—giving himself, and consequently Williams, complete artistic control. For his own part, Williams neither understood nor cared about contract negotiations, and the fact that everything turned out so well for him was entirely the result of Kazan's maneuvering. (Kazan would later call *Streetcar* "the best play I've ever done.")

Selznick wanted Williams to come to Hollywood to discuss the play, and on his return to California he was treated as a celebrity. She made sure he had the best of everything. He had never been especially impressed by Hollywood ostentation, but in a letter to his grandfather he gushed about everything that was happening. Part of the mission in Hollywood was to network at cocktail parties and brokered meetings, but it was also necessary to find an actor to play the key role of Blanche DuBois. Jessica Tandy was selected; she had performed in a number of plays on Broadway already, as well as a few films, and she would later be hailed by the press for her embodiment of her character in *Streetcar*.

After the Hollywood expedition, Williams returned to Cape Cod to rest. Kazan sent to him a young man from New York as a possible addition to the cast. The young actor had been given bus money, but he'd pocketed this and hitched a ride instead; on arriving at Williams' cottage, he fixed the broken plumbing and the electricity before even reading from the script. Margo Jones, who was there at the time, was ebullient. "Get Kazan on the phone right away!" she exclaimed. "This is the greatest reading I've ever heard—in or outside of Texas!" The actor whose reading had inspired her reaction was Marlon Brando. His charismatic presence so affected Williams, too, that Kazan received "an ecstatic call from [the] author, in a voice near hysteria" and knew that "Brando had overwhelmed him."

For the first time, Williams actually enjoyed play rehearsals. Working with the brilliant and soft-spoken Kazan was a joy. The director understood actors, allowing them the freedom to use whatever was at their disposal to sculpt their character. He worked closely with Williams, asking many questions and suggesting changes, never demanding them, along the way. Expenses for the show were shouldered by a number of celebrities, including Irene Selznick, who put up $25,000. It was decided the play would go on tour before opening in New York, and the plan worked beautifully; audiences in Philadelphia loved it, as did those in dreaded Boston.

The play opened at the Barrymore Theater in New York on December 3, 1947 and was an instant sensation. It would go on to win the New York Drama Critics' Circle Award, the Donaldson Award, and the Pulitzer Prize—the first play to receive all three. Williams used the money from the Pulitzer Prize to establish a graduate scholarship in his name at the University of Missouri, his alma mater.

Williams took little if any pleasure in this, continuing to battle his familiar personal demons of fear and insecurity, those that would taint the pleasure of even his greatest achievements. He was afraid, too, that getting too comfortable would diminish his creativity. At the height of all the media attention, then, and as he had done before, he quietly disappeared—this time aboard a ship bound for Europe.

During the time of the production of *Streetcar*, Dakin Williams, now a practicing attorney, was asked by Edwina Williams to enact her legal separation from Cornelius. In the contract, Edwina received two hundred shares of Cornelius' holdings in the shoe company, along with his interest in the house. There was never a divorce, nor would they ever see each other again. Edwina had found a certain resolution: "I was happy to have my freedom, the walls of the house had resounded with wrath for too many years and now there was peace at long last." Williams' father left St. Louis to live with his sister Ella in Knoxville. (After a few years, she too would turn him away; "I'm poor, and I need your board money," she would say, "but ... I'd rather starve to death than live with you.")

Now that his mother was emancipated from the almost demonic presence of his father, Williams made a point of including her in as many of his events as possible, such as cast parties and the debuts of his plays. Ever the *flâneur* in Europe, he ended up in Rome and was entranced by the ancient Italian city. In a letter to his mother he said, "To me it is the place where I find the sun not only in the sky, where Italy also keeps it, but in the heart of the people." He rented a small apartment there and worked on revising *Summer and Smoke* and writing another new play. The longer he remained with the natives of this city, the more he wanted to write about them, but realized he hadn't the knowledge or expertise to do so. Instead he created a plot about an American in Italy; this was the seed for the novel *The Roman Spring of Mrs. Stone*, which would be published a few years after his return to the United States.

Plans were being made for *The Glass Menagerie* to open in London, but Williams had his doubts that his work would be accepted there. Nevertheless, his mother and Dakin were invited to attend the pre-miere—as was his grandfather, who couldn't be persuaded. Edwina and Dakin attended the opening night of the play at the Royal Theater in the Haymarket of London, along with several British dignitaries and members of the royal family. Despite many imploring telegrams, Williams remained in Rome and was conspicuously absent not only from the performance but also from the cast party afterward that was hosted by Lady Sibyl Colfax. Williams was a confirmed Anglophobe, by this time either bored or intimidated by all the hobnobbing, and his instincts were right about the play, which closed before the end of its first run.

Back in the States, Margo Jones had become the producer and director of *Summer and Smoke*, now scheduled to open at the Music Box Theater in New York on October 6, 1948; Williams did attend this one, and he asked Carson McCullers to accompany him to the cast party. The reviews of the play were so very negative that Williams decided to follow the cast party with a "bad-notice party," inviting many of the most notorious literary critics of the time. (If this was meant to influence the opinions of his detractors, the ploy failed, for the show would close before Christmas of that year.)

FRANK MERLO

Also prior to the play's demise, Williams met and became involved romantically with twenty-six-year-old Frank Merlo, a working-class Navy veteran. Merlo was detail-oriented, and Williams, of course, was not, and the two became a happy kind of "odd couple." For the first time in many years, Williams could attend solely to his writing, for Merlo did the laundry, the cooking, the packing, the cleaning, and even drove Williams wherever he wanted to go.

Williams took Merlo with him on his next trip to Rome, but he was depressed over the failure of *Summer and Smoke* and treated Merlo poorly. Side trips were taken to North Africa, London, and Paris, all while Williams worked on his new novel, The *Roman Spring of Mrs. Stone*. He complained that it was difficult to write well in Italy, as his time there now reminded him of his days of torpor in Hollywood. While in Rome, he spent a good deal of time with his friend Anna Magnani, an actor at the zenith of her success who had the means to entertain lavishly. Since Magnani was Roman and Merlo Sicilian, Williams was able to use them in developing the characters in his novel. He placed Italian characters in the United States, too, in *The Rose Tattoo*, a play about a Sicilian community on the Gulf Coast that Williams called his "love-play to the world."

Williams' friend Gilbert Maxwell thought *The Rose Tattoo* was preoccupied with the symbolism of the word *rose*. References to roses and their color, he thought, and attributions to the characters themselves, appeared with distracting frequency throughout the work; the main character even called her husband "a rose of a man." Williams wanted Kazan to direct this play, but Kazan was tied up with two upcoming film projects. Throughout the writing of this play, too, Williams had envisioned Magnani as the central character, but she felt her English wasn't adequate for a stage drama, in which she might have to improvise at any given moment—and backed out. (She would later play Serafina in the film version of the play and receive an Academy Award for her performance.) The play opened in New York at the Martin Beck Theater to mixed reviews—most critics, like Maxwell, thought the *rose* technique awkward and overstated—but the box office was boosted when several Hearst papers praised the play. While *The Rose Tattoo* won the Antoinette Perry award (the Tony), it would never see the popularity of Williams' other plays.

Williams began spending more time in Key West, taking his grandfather there as often as possible. (Reverend Dakin and Frank Merlo liked each other and got along well.) He rented a three-bedroom house and later purchased a home, which grew into a compound with a pool and a guest house. As he grew wealthier, he discovered that more and more of his assets were vanishing into federal taxes. His money also went habitually to any of his friends who asked for it—and to many who didn't. Wood suggested that he donate to the Authors League Fund, established for impoverished professional writers, to "kill two birds with one stone"; in this way, the money he spent to help his friends would be tax-deductible. He also spent vast sums on his sister Rose, hoping to emancipate her from the state-run sanitarium in which she had been living. He wanted to place her in a private home and was able to install her in a managed-care facility where she would have her own cottage on the wooded grounds of the hospital.

The decade of the 1950s began with the publication of Williams' *The Roman Spring of Mrs. Stone*, coincident with the release of the film version of *The Glass Menagerie*. Sales of the novel were meager, to Williams' disappointment, and the screenplay for *The Glass Menagerie*— whose ending had been made more "upbeat" by film executives in Hollywood—left much to be desired. While the film netted a substantial profit, Williams was far from satisfied with the finished product. (He called it "the most awful travesty of the play I've ever seen ... horribly mangled by the people who did the film-script.") He and Wood determined to be more wary on the next screenplay, which turned out to be for the play *A Streetcar Named Desire*. They asked Kazan to adapt the play for film, and Kazan agreed. Production began in 1951 with much of the cast from the original stage play. Throughout the months of production, Williams reworked the play that earlier Wood had told him not to show to anyone. The earlier version entitled *Ten Blocks on the Camino Real* had been shortened to *Camino Real*. The play was pure fantasy, and Williams soon learned that convincing anyone to try fantasy on Broadway was tough going. Fortunately, by this time Kazan had faith in Williams and his work and was willing to direct the play.

Despite Kazan's work, *Camino Real*, which opened in New York in March of 1953, earned savage reviews and closed after only sixty performances. The critic Brooks Atkinson saw the play as superbly written but derided Williams' "increasing preoccupation with degeneracy, corruption and horror." Because the play represented a major shift in Williams' thematic approach, Williams was extremely disappointed by the vitriolic response.

To take his mind off of this, Williams agreed to direct a play for his old companion Don Windham—with whom he'd shied away from collaborating since *You Touched Me!*. The new work, *The Starless Air*, was slated for an opening in Houston, but there were many squabbles between Williams and Windham and eventually Williams became discouraged enough to resign as director. The backers felt that the play would go nowhere without Williams' name, and the play never made it to New York; the incident drove Williams and Windham further apart. In June of 1953, Williams returned to Europe. While there, he began developing the plot for *Three Players of a Summer Game*, which focused on life in the South and the complexities of the family unit. As it developed over the following year, this story became one of Williams' masterworks, *Cat on a Hot Tin Roof*.

KAZAN DIRECTS *CAT ON A HOT TIN ROOF*

Cat on a Hot Tin Roof brought Williams and Elia Kazan together again, but this play would strain their relationship severely; each continued to respect the other's work, but there were many differences of opinion during the play's production. Kazan's ideas for the character of Big

Daddy, for example, never meshed with the playwright's vision, and a compromise was reached that in Williams' view could never suffice for the original ending.

During rehearsals for *Cat*, Williams received word that his grandfather Dakin had died. He interrupted his work and rushed to St. Louis, arriving at the house with a large box containing a blanket of flowers to be placed on the casket—a massive array of violets and white carnations, his grandfather's favorite flowers, in the shape of a St. Andrew's cross. Reverend Dakin was buried in Waynesville, Ohio, where he had been raised, next to his wife. Williams established a memorial room in his grandfather's honor at the theological school of the University of the South, his grandfather's alma mater. The Reverend's effect on his grandson's life had been incalculable, and his loss was difficult for Williams to bear.

Cat on a Hot Tin Roof opened at the Morosco Theater in New York on March 24, 1955. It would become Williams' longest-running Broadway play, eventually sold to MGM for $750,000 and made into a film starring Elizabeth Taylor and Paul Newman; it would earn its author yet another New York Critics' Circle Award and his second Pulitzer Prize. At first Williams had no idea of the play's success, for, as was his habit at such times, he had first upset everyone around him and then fled the country, again for Rome. Among the victims of this particular bout of anxiety was Audrey Wood, his agent and dear friend, who by now was tiring of his idiosyncrasies—and especially his regular eruptions of temper. Whether he handled success or failure with less aplomb was unclear; he seemed unable to enjoy the success of *Cat* and, moreover, seemed haunted by it. Around this time, Williams began to support himself with stimulants more powerful than alcohol and black coffee, and his dependency on narcotics grew.

The Stressors Take Their Toll

Battle of Angels—now rewritten as *Orpheus Descending*—found no warmer welcome in 1957 than it had found in 1940. It closed after 68 performances in the U.S., though it did well in Russia and would run there for seven years. The combination of the disappointment over this play and the emotional turmoil surrounding the death of his father, which also took place in that year, drove Williams to seek psychotherapy. He would say later that the analysis had helped him to know his true nature; but at the time it offered no solutions. The death of Cornelius Williams affected Williams more than he had imagined it would, for both he and his brother Dakin had grown to pity their father, despite Cornelius' often ruthless nature. While Edwina noted in her memoirs that neither son had wept at the death of their father, both contradicted the account. And Williams faced two more important deaths in the following years: Diana Barrymore, "1942's Most Sensational New Screen Personality" and a close friend, committed suicide in January of 1960 after a brief and tragic life; and a few years later, Frank Merlo was diagnosed with cancer and, after a lingering and painful illness, he died in 1963. Merlo's death sent Williams into the deepest depression he'd ever known. All the while he took pills for sleeping, pills for waking up, and pills to settle his nerves. Wherever he went, the pills went with him. His dependencies became more and more marked; he would later refer to the 1960s as his "Stoned Age."

The project demanding most of his attention at this time was a work that was very close to his heart, *The Night of the Iguana*. The play, whose setting was modeled on the beach at Acapulco where he had met Paul and Jane Bowles after his alienation from Kip Kiernan, revolved around an older priest; Williams based this character loosely on his grandfather, Reverend Dakin. When the tour of the play started, Williams traveled with the group, working on rewrites daily. For eight weeks, he worked long hours, often without sleep. The reviews on tour were mixed, so no one was sure how the play would be received in New York; all were surprised when it earned another New York Drama Critics' Circle Award. Williams' photo appeared on the cover of *Time* with the headline "The Greatest Living Playwright in the English-Speaking World." The film version would be shot on location in Mexico in 1964, and it too would become a marked success.

In the spring of 1963, Edwina Williams surprised her son—unpleasantly—by releasing her own book about him, entitled *Remember Me to Tom*. Williams was not at all happy with the book, especially with the parts about Cornelius, who was no longer present to defend himself against her assertions. The co-writer, Lucy Freeman, admitted that the book had been written hurriedly. During this same year, Williams' play *The Milk Train Doesn't Stop Here Anymore* was panned by the New York critics. When he ran off to Key West to recuperate from this latest disappointment, he learned that his house had been opened as a tourist attraction. He then left for Europe, where he learned that his New York apartment had been burglarized. Nothing was going right.

After returning home, Williams took the recommendation of a friend and visited a doctor, who gave him an injection of an amphetamine that was legal at the time. The effect was euphoric; it cleared his head and enabled him to write again. He was told the drug could be purchased as pills, and he acquired it. The trouble with his self-medication, as he would later admit, was that he unwisely took the pills in combination with alcohol—and the effect of this methodology was a style writing that was much more surrealistic, implying the drug, alluding to the drug. As one biographer describes it, Williams' work of this period "is speed all the way through, and the trouble with speed is the letdown."

In 1966, Williams met Bill Glavin, who took the place of Frank Merlo in his life in a positive way—looking after the details of quotidian life. Like others who knew Williams well, Bill was awestruck by his dedication to his work. He also recalled that during this time Williams was becoming addicted to his daily speed injections. One clear indication of Williams' dependence came on a trip they took to Spain together; on their arrival, Williams realized his "medicine" was missing and insisted frantically that they fly immediately back to New York. He had left the bottle on the dresser, and by that time it was obvious that he couldn't be without it. Friends were noticing distinct changes in Williams' behavior by 1968. He was seldom present at the rehearsals of his play *The Seven Descents of Myrtle*, and when he *was* present, his manner was erratic, he was on edge, he sweated profusely, and his speech was often garbled. The play was an absolute failure, and his "crackup" (his own choice of terms) came at last in the following year.

Early in 1969, Dakin persuaded his brother to convert to Roman Catholicism, a move that may have been more for Dakin's peace of mind than for his own. In that spring, Williams' play *In the Bar of a Tokyo Hotel* opened in New York, but it closed soon after. The new faith was not helping; Williams had begun to feel that everyone had turned against him, and as the drugs eroded his mind he would sleep up to 17 hours a day. His famous discipline was a thing of the past. He was often incoherent, and his hands constantly shook. He and Bill Glavin had parted company on bad terms, and Williams was once again alone.

Back home in Key West, Williams fell while carrying a pot of boiling coffee and burned his shoulder badly. His brother Dakin was called to the scene, and after surveying what a mess his brother was in, he had him committed to a hospital in St. Louis. The period that followed was a terrible time for both of them. The drugs were taken from him, and, he went into convulsions, nearly dying once from a heart attack. For a man who all his life had feared slipping into insanity like his sister, the entire experience was a nightmare. Williams was kept confined for three months, during the first few days of which he was too furious even to see Dakin, and was released in time for Christmas. He spent the holidays at his mother's house in St. Louis, where he reportedly watched the television film of *The Roman Spring of Mrs. Stone*. Many of Williams' friends would later affirm that Dakin's actions probably had saved his life; but Williams would never fully forgive his younger brother for committing him to the hospital, or for the treatment he had received while he was there. It would be another year or so before the relationship would even begin to heal.

AFTER THE HOSPITAL

Everyone, even Williams, felt he had much improved since his hospitalization. He was off drugs and drinking only white wine, and he was once again writing every day. Williams broke off his longstanding relationship with Audrey Wood in 1971—he'd been attacking her verbally, often accusing her of no longer believing in him—and took on another agent, Bill Barnes, who worked with the temperamental playwright as well as he could. Williams' play *Small Craft Warnings*, originally entitled *Confessional*, expressed overtly his homosexuality and the sadness and loneliness that his desires had brought him. He'd not had a successful play for more than a decade, so, with renewed energy, he did his best to promote *Small Craft Warnings*, even acting in it himself. His efforts paid off; the play enjoyed a six-month run and turned a profit.

Doubleday Publishing commissioned Williams to write his memoirs in 1975, paying him an advance of $50,000. The result was no masterpiece; he had permitted Doubleday to edit the book as it wished, Williams said, and the published book was half as long as the original manuscript had been. Like his mother's book before him, it had been written quickly and without careful thought or much attention to detail. He'd rambled through many of its pages, and the events recounted in the book were sometimes inconsistent with the dates he gave for them. Still, for all its faults, the book was eagerly received, and Williams signed copies for four hours straight at Doubleday's bookstore on Fifth Avenue.

Williams had often said he wanted to live a more secluded life, but even in the wake of his published memoirs, that was unlikely to happen. In 1976, Williams granted permission to a Canadian filmmaker, Harry Rasky, to film a documentary about his life. The sensitive and talented Rasky captured Williams' very essence; filmed on location in Key West and in New Orleans, the documentary featured many places where the playwright had lived and worked, and the segments that showed Williams reading portions of his plays were especially moving. The film proved immensely popular in Canada but less so in the United States, where Williams was no longer in vogue. It was eventually aired, but it wouldn't be in demand until after Williams' death a few years later.

The realization of Williams' vision of a private life was deferred even further in the same year by Donald Windham's publication of their correspondence. Williams was shocked, for he'd never imagined in writing the letters that they would one day be available for public viewing.

THE WORK CONTINUES

Still, his professional writing continued unabated, if less successfully than in the past. He became fascinated with F. Scott Fitzgerald and Zelda Fitzgerald, and decided to write a play about their lives. *Clothes for a Summer Hotel* opened in 1980, around the time of Williams' 69th birthday, but the play hardly survived past its debut. He lost nearly $500,000 on the production, and some said it was the worst thing he'd ever written. A few months later, he received word that his mother had died, and he and Dakin prepared services for her at Christ Church Cathedral in St. Louis; it is also around this time that Williams set aside a portion of his estate to ensure that the unfortunate Rose would be cared for until the end of her days. Soon afterward, Williams and Dakin traveled to the White House together, where President Jimmy Carter presented Williams with the Presidential Medal of Freedom, the highest honor a civilian can receive from the government of the United States.

It was toward the end of 1980 that Williams began what would be his last play; *A House Not Meant to Stand*, an exploration of the conditions of society as Williams saw them, opened in Chicago to favorable reviews.

Williams had often said he would work right up until the moment of his death, and so he did; he died abruptly, choking on a small plastic bottlecap after a night of heavy drinking, between February 24 and 25, 1983. He was alone in his hotel room in New York City at the time—at the Hotel Elysée, a name reminiscent of the tenement in *A Streetcar Named Desire*. He had said that he wanted his body to be sewn into a white bag and dropped into the sea near where Hart Crane had drowned, but his brother overrode his wishes and buried Williams in St. Louis, a city Williams loathed, for Dakin thought it right that such a popular personality be buried where those who loved his work could visit his grave. And he may have had a point; *The New York Times* summarized Williams' effect on American culture: "Tennessee Williams ... left many mourners: strangers who for forty years depended on him for the most magical evenings in American theater."

Tennessee Williams produced dozens of short plays and screenplays, two novels, a novella, 60 short stories, more than 100 poems, and an autobiography; he proved that, contrary to popular belief, a play of quiet emotion, written with bracing poetic diction, could compete with the commercial productions of Broadway. When asked what it was like to be a writer, he said, "It is like being free.... To be free is to have achieved your life ... [and] it means to be a voyager here and there.... It means the freedom of being." But like success, this "freedom of being" seems to have had a dark side for Williams: "I live like a gypsy," he said. "I am a fugitive. No place seems tenable to me for long ... not even my own skin."

Williams seems never to have been comfortable with himself or his work. His shyness was overpowering, and he was often lonely and afraid, alienated, sometimes even disoriented. But he considered the difficulties of his life the cost of writing as he did, out of his own personal pain. "I have never valued work, created work, that was not personal," he once said. "I think you have to use your life—what you have experienced and felt—as the material for your creative work. Otherwise, you're just manufacturing something that is not deeply rooted in you at all."

AIMEE LABRIE

An Introduction to Tennessee Williams

One of the most moving moments in Tennessee Williams' *A Streetcar Named Desire* occurs in the last act of the play. The fading Southern belle Blanche DuBois, led away to an asylum at last, reaches for the doctor who has come to escort her; leaning on his arm, she utters her famous last lines: "Whoever you are—I have always depended on the kindness of strangers." On stage, the poker game that started the play begins again. Blanche's sister, Stella, stands holding her newborn boy, torn between Blanche and her own husband, Stanley. He kneels at her feet, slowly unbuttoning her blouse, and murmuring, "Now honey. Now, love. Now, now, love...." As the lights fade, the tinny music from the bar on the corner plays, "Blue Piano," the song that opens the first act. As the curtain falls, the trajectories of the characters' lives are faintly visible: Stella and Stanley will live out their days in the cramped rooms in Elysian Fields, and Blanche will remain trapped in the world she has invented, her "beautiful dream," where beaux still call with flowers and the mirror reflects a youthful face. It is moments like this that have earned Tennessee Williams his place as one of the foremost American playwrights of the twentieth century; *Time* even once called him "the greatest living playwright in the English-speaking world."

A large part of the scholarship dedicated to Williams discusses the various ways in which his plays relate to occurrences in his life. Philip Kolin's *Tennessee Williams* devotes a section in each chapter to the biographical context of Williams' writing. But contending that a writer's

work is autobiographical is like contending that Southerners come from
the South. The more interesting question to ask is to what degree the
writing itself served Williams.

Williams never denied his attraction to using writing as a way to
process the events of his own life. In his autobiography, *Memoirs*, he
explains that "the theatre and I found each other for better or for
worse.... I know [writing] is the only thing that saved my life." (42)
"[T]he point is," he writes, "I already knew that writing was my life and
its failing would be my death." (44) And his foreword to *Sweet Bird of
Youth* elaborates:

> ... I discovered writing as an escape from a world of reality in
> which I felt acutely uncomfortable. It immediately became
> my place of retreat, my cave, my refuge. From what? From
> being called a sissy by neighborhood kids, and Miss Nancy by
> my father, because I would rather read books in my
> grandfather's large and classical library than play marbles and
> baseball and other normal kid games, a result of a severe
> childhood illness and of excessive attachment to the female
> members of my family, who had coaxed me back into life.
> (151)

He began to write plays in his youth; he continued in part because
of his success and the encouragement he received from audiences,
inconsistent though that encouragement may have been. He produced
63 plays in his lifetime: 24 full-length and 39 shorter. He also published
two books of poetry, two novels, an autobiography, four books of short
stories, and a collection of essays. Many of his longer plays were
expansions of short stories or one-act works, and he was constantly in
the process of revision or rewriting. (*Battle of Angels*, for instance, his first
play to be produced, was later transformed into *Orpheus Descending*.)

THEMES IN WILLIAMS' WORK

Williams' primary thematic obsessions, if he can be said to have
obsessions, are sexuality and aggression; some critics have called his use
of these grotesque sensationalism. Sexuality and aggression run through
Williams' plays either as a palpable tension or as one that boils beneath

the surface, threatening to erupt at any moment. The injuries that take place onstage consist of physical blows, the destruction of property, and the intimation of sexual violence or degradation—menace. The scene in *Kingdom of Earth/The Seven Descents of Myrtle* that most unsettled or disgusted audiences occurs when Chicken sits, legs spread, in front of Myrtle, "the whore":

> MYRTLE: Wouldn't you be more comf'tble in a chair?
> CHICKEN: I wouldn' be as close to you.—I'm right in front of you now.
> MYRTLE: That's a—high—table. I have to strain my neck to look in your face.
> CHICKEN [*with a slow, savage grin*]:—You don't have to look in my face, my face ain't all they is to me ... [VI, 693]

Offstage, the violence is even darker. Val Xavier is lynched; Sebastian's flesh is torn off in chunks by starving children; Rosario is assassinated; Chance Wayne and another man are castrated. The sexual aspects of Williams' plays can be as destructive. Many of the female characters, such as Alma in *Summer and Smoke* and Karen Stone in *The Roman Spring of Mrs. Stone*, end up in pursuit of debauched physical pleasure with multiple partners to erase the loss of the hope of love.

The sexual content of Williams' plays can be traced in most of his work. When *Battle of Angels* was first produced, for example, theatergoers were aghast at its representation of desire, passion, and infidelity. In this play, the renegade stranger Val Xavier meets Myra, the proprietor of a candy shop, whose husband, Jab, is upstairs (and offstage) dying. The attraction between Val and Myra is evident from the start, and they eventually slip into the storage room together to consummate their desire. In the same play, the alcoholic Cassandra becomes the prototype for Blanche DuBois—highly sexually charged and in need of male "companionship." Unlike Blanche, however, Cassandra is no shrinking violet. She frames her desire for Val openly as a kind of sympathy:

> Why don't you come with me? You an' me, we belong to the fugitive kind. We live on motion. Think of it, al. Nothing but motion, motion, mile after mile, keeping up with the

wind, or even faster! Doesn't that make you hungry? [III, 257]

In a similar fashion, Williams' male characters often embody a highly charged masculinity that borders on the animalistic. Stanley Kowalski, for instance, seems largely defined by his sexual urges and a primal need to dominate. Just before he rapes his sister-in-law, Blanche, he growls "Oh! So you want some roughhouse! All right, let's have some rough-house.... Tiger-tiger! Drop the bottle-top! Drop it! We've had this date with each other from the beginning!" (III, xi) Val Xavier in *Orpheus Descending*—the rewritten *Battle of Angels*—rides into a strange town like a contemporary Messiah, wearing a snakeskin jacket, carrying a guitar, and causing the women in town to spend more time in the shoestore than usual. In *Cat on a Hot Tin Roof*, the three central male figures—Brick Pollitt, his brother, and their powerful, authoritative father, Big Daddy—all are intimidating in one way or another.

In some cases, however, the overt masculinity becomes a mask for sexual ambiguity or homosexuality. In *Cat on a Hot Tin Roof*, for example, the former football hero Brick cannot commit sexually to his beautiful, voluptuous wife, Maggie. He turns to alcohol for the solace of its "click" and broods over the combination of residual anger and sexual ambiguity that prevents their union. The highly sexual Maggie, determined both to repair her relationship with the man she loves and to bear the child that will secure Big Daddy's favor, demands that Brick tell her why they aren't sleeping together. When Brick won't confront her, she tries to provoke him by insinuating that Brick's cherished former teammate wanted more than friendship from him:

> MARGARET: ... [I]t was only Skipper that harbored even any unconscious desire for anything not perfectly pure between you two.... You organized the Dixie Stars that fall, so you could keep on bein' teammates forever! But something was not right with it! Me included! Between you two. Skipper began hittin' the bottle.... We drank together that night, all night in the bar of the Blackstone and when cold day was comin' up over the Lake an' we were comin' out drunk to take a dizzy look at it, I said, "SKIPPER! STOP LOVIN' MY HUSBAND OR TELL

HIM HE'S GOT TO LET YOU ADMIT IT TO HIM!"—one way or another!

One of the most startling aspects of the play, or the most progressive, is the degree of Maggie's acceptance of Brick's possible homosexuality. She's not looking to lord it over him; she just wants him to admit it, to save them all from continuing the game of denial:

> BRICK: Man has one great good true thing in his life. One great good thing which is true!—I had friendship with Skipper.—You're naming it dirty!
> MARGARET: I'm not naming it dirty! I am naming it clean.

Williams' ability to create a paradigm for alternative sexual object choice is highly unusual for the conservatism of his time, but it seems that in *Cat* Williams sought a greater understanding of his own sexual identity. *Memoirs* reads like a catalogue of sexual conquests, but this openness is part of what Williams struggled for throughout his life, and he revisits desire again and again in his work. Kolin posits that Williams' later plays express homosexuality more openly because, through several channels, he had come to terms more effectively with his own homosexual tendencies. (184)

As George-Michael Sarote points out in *Staging Difference: Cultural Pluralism in American Theater and Drama*,

> Tennessee Williams' "difference," that of gay artists, always finds its way onto the stage, after having sustained transformations required by the genre and time. The majority of his plays present characters that are too sensitive and/or too sensual to be fully adapted to their conventional social milieu. They sooner or later clash with reality, with the hostility of normal emotion. (10)

However, this same treatment of homosexuality in later years was received with less enthusiasm, perhaps because Williams' reputation as a writer had lost strength or because the subject matter was too graphic even for audiences of the 1960s. *Suddenly Last Summer* and *Two-Character/Out Cry* both suggest repressed incestuous lust. *Suddenly Last*

Summer tells of a woman whose son has been killed in the Galapagos Islands. What this lady, Violet Venable, does not want to recognize is that he was murdered and eaten by the young men he had been attempting to seduce. Philip Kolin notes in *Tennessee Williams* that "most reviewers have ... unfavorably noted the plays' more explicit, indeed, scatological, treatment of sexuality, and especially homosexuality." (185)

Still, the *central* thematic concern in Williams' plays is the isolation of individuals who are trapped in desperate circumstances dictated by social class, failed dreams, familial constraints, or the loss of power or beauty. Their only escape becomes to disengage from the real world and to construct their own realities. *The Glass Menagerie* presents the most obvious example of this. Set in a post-Depression America on the brink of World War II, *Menagerie* is narrated by Tom Wingfield, who looks back on a climactic evening from years before. Tom is a young sea merchant who lives in a cramped tenement in St. Louis with his flighty mother and crippled sister, both of whom he supports alone. His only escape from the burden of responsibility is to lose himself in adventure stories at a movie theater. Like her son, Amanda Wingfield ignores the precariousness of their financial situation; she dreams of her years as a debutante in Blue Mountain, Mississippi. Laura's acute shyness keeps her from finishing secretary school or participating in social events. She has never been kissed or had a date. Her solace is the collection of glass animals that she cares for solicitously. Though the members of the family live together, they all suffer from the need to escape reality, and this desire keeps them from fully connecting with each other or anyone else. For Tom, the pressure to take care of the family is too great, and finally he must abandon the others.

In some of Williams' plays, the desire to flee lonely and desperate lives leads to devastating results. The rape of Blanche DuBois by her brother-in-law is precipitated in part by her stubborn insistence on living in an imaginary world; and Stanley's very real assault pushes her into madness. Williams explained that he understood the isolation felt by his characters; he admitted in *Conversations with Tennessee Williams* that his characters are "people I know." And for him, this was necessary: "Perhaps that limits me as an artist," he said, "but nevertheless I couldn't create believable characters if I moved outside of that world." (82) The work was an affirmation, too—not only of individualism, but also of community and compassion: "I have always had a deep feeling for the mystery in life and essentially my plays have been an effort to explore the beauty and meaning in the confusion of living." (28)

Everywhere in Williams' plays is the ticking of clocks, the feeling that time is slipping away. Roger Boxhill points in *Tennessee Williams* to the implication of time or its passage in many of Williams' titles: *Summer and Smoke, Suddenly Last Summer, Clothes for a Summer Hotel, The Roman Spring of Mrs. Stone, A Lovely Sunday for Creve Coeur, The Night of the Iguana, Period of Adjustment,* The *Milk Train Doesn't Stop Here Anymore,* and *A Streetcar Named Desire.* (28) This obsession with time may be linked to one of Williams' well-known personality traits—his constant belief that he was dying. Even at the age of forty, Williams was preparing deathbed speeches and setting his affairs, but —although he did suffer from a nearly fatal case of diphtheria as a child and struggle with cataracts and appendicitis later in life—the only real impediment to his health was his drinking, drug abuse, and relative promiscuity. He fought his addictions but remained dependent on the numbness they brought him, even to the moment of his death.

The thematic emphasis on the slippery passage of time is Williams' way of circling around, or perhaps of confronting, the fear of growing older. Like Williams himself, though, his characters rarely succeed in convincing themselves that the past is within their grasp. Blanche DuBois, the character most known for her controlling of the lighting and hiding behind veils, may exemplify Williams' wish to keep time at bay—but neither she nor he, ultimately, can stop the ticking of the clock.

If these "thematic obsessions" can be seen as parallels to Williams' own life, though, then no discussion of them can be complete without the mention of his religious references. In *Kingdom of the Earth,* references are made to biblical moments such as Noah and the Flood, and the title itself recalls the Biblical phrase "Blessed are the meek, for they will inherit the earth." (Matthew 5:5) Other plays are set on Christian holidays (*Period of Adjustment, Mutilated,* and *Moony's Kid* on Christmas; *Sweet Bird of Youth* and *Orpheus* on Easter). Summer and Smoke takes its primary image from the stone angel in the center of the stage with the words "Eternity" etched into it. Boxhill concludes, perhaps with some labor, that the devouring of Sebastian Venable can be related to "an indirect allusion to the Eucharist." (130) It has been noted many times that part of what shaped Williams was his puritanical upbringing; his work does tend, speaking reductively, toward battles between good and evil.

Archetypal Characters

Williams employs archetypal characters that reappear consistently, always slightly altered, within his work. Ren Draya discusses these in his essay "The Fiction of Tennessee Williams":

> One favorite Williams figure [is] the earthy middle-aged woman.... Another recurring character is the handsome (often dark) young man, sensual and compelling.... In contrast to these sexual beings, Williams often portrays a person (a woman, usually) repressed and fearful. (653)

> The qualities of repression and fear are parts of the dominant Williams motif of the outcast: the emotional or physical cripple who suffers intense loneliness and hunger for love and acceptance. Both the 1967 slapstick tragedy *The Mutilated* and the early story "One Arm" explicitly label physical deformities. Laura in "Portrait of a Girl in Glass" is shy and secretive, but in the play [*The Glass Menagerie*] Williams adds a visible deformity (a lame foot) to emphasize the girl's estrangement from society. (654)

Although his characters fight valiantly to escape their constraints, it seems inevitable that, in Williams' vision at least, they are destined to fail. Again and again, Williams' work underscores that human creatures are *trapped*. In an autobiographical context, his plays can be read as attempts to correct his own desire to take shelter in a world that is judgmental and lonely.

His aging female characters relate particularly to the theme of the passage of time; they descend into fantasy instead of recognizing they have lost much of their attractiveness and charm and are on the verge of sinking into social invisibility. Certainly, Blanche epitomizes this characteristic—in the dim lighting with which she surrounds herself, in her airs of a Southern belle on the lost plantation of Belle Reve, and in her pathological hunger for male attention. Amanda Wingfield, too, remembers earlier days, particularly one time when she had seventeen male "callers" at one time. Violet Venable, the matron in *Suddenly Last Summer*, clings to the memory of her dead son. The ex-singer in

Gnadiges Fraulein takes comfort in paging through an old scrapbook containing her press releases. The no-longer-attractive actor Mrs. Stone in *The Roman Spring of Mrs. Stone* seeks the company of a young male prostitute, Paolo, to restore her belief that she can still attract a man despite her dyed hair and the wrinkles appearing on her face. However, she cannot escape the memory of her last failed performance—in which she attempted to play fourteen-year old Juliet in *Romeo and Juliet*. Like Mrs. Stone, Amanda Wingfield, and the rest of Williams' characters of this type, the central figures in *Sweet Bird of Youth* want to return to what they remember as a happier time. The main male figure, Chance Wayne, has returned to St. Cloud to claim Heavenly Finley, his first love. His wish is destined to fail from the beginning, but Chance refuses to see that too much time has passed, and too much damage been done, for him to win her affection again. His female companion, Princess (the once-famous screen star Alexandra del Lago) also wants to return to her youth and fame. But such a fight against time in this play, as in Williams' other work, is inevitably useless. The dialogue between Chance and Princess at the end of *Sweet Bird of Youth* underscores this point:

> PRINCESS: Look, a shepherd boy's leading a flock—What an
>   old country, timeless.—Look—
> *[The sound of a clock ticking is heard, louder and louder.]*
> CHANCE: No, listen. I didn't know there was a clock in this
>   room.
> PRINCESS: I guess there's a clock in every room people live
>   in....
> CHANCE: It goes tick-tick, it's quieter than your heart-beat,
>   but it's slow dynamite, a gradual explosion, blasting the
>   world we lived in to burnt-out pieces...Time—who could
>   beat it, who could defeat it ever? Maybe some saints and
>   heroes, but not Chance Wayne. I lived on something,
>   that—time?
> PRINCESS: Yes, time.
> CHANCE: ... Gnaws away, like a rat gnaws off its own foot
>   caught in a trap, and then, with its foot gnawed off and the
>   rat set free, it couldn't run, couldn't go, bled and died ...
> *[The clock ticking fades away.]* (III, 235–36)

Poetic Language and Stage Technique

Williams has been called one of the most poetic writers of the stage, perhaps because of his lyrical control of language. Unfortunately, his *Memoirs*, though humorous and self-deprecating, shows very little of his aesthetic. However, as he aged and his plays became a product for mass consumption, he seems to have become too self-aware; and his writing exemplifies his inability to lose himself in the prose. Norman J. Fedder, in his essay "Tennessee Williams' Dramatic Techniques," finds Williams uniquely talented in this arena:

> Williams' language has been unequaled in the American theater in its ability to be both conversationally idiomatic and poetically vivid—true to both the surface appearance and the inner truth. Williams has brought poetry back to the theater to a more significant degree than T.S. Eliot, Christopher Frey, and Maxwell Anderson, but hardly seeming to do so. (234)

Francis Donahue seems to agree:

> In his dialogue, Williams achieves a colloquial pungency, which is realistic and poetic at the same time. His heroines ... can often indulge in a type of rhetoric which may set them off from their surroundings. His heroes generally speak a cadenced slang which is considered sensitive realism. Overall, his dialogue is supple and hard-hitting, characterized by a fine Southern quality. (225)

But if his language was particular, as Fedder and Donahue contend, then his setting requirements were certainly no less so. His production notes for *Summer and Smoke*, for example, almost depart from the realm of the feasible, becoming more of an impression than a direction:

> During the day scenes the sky should be a pure and intense blue (like the sky of Italy as it is so faithfully represented in the religious paintings of the Renaissance) and costumes should be selected to form dramatic color contrasts to this

intense blue which the figure stand against (color harmonies and other visual effects are tremendously important).

In the night scenes, the more familiar constellations, such as Orion and the Great Bear and the Pleiades, are clearly projected on the night sky, and above them, splashed across the top of the cyclorama, is the nebulous radiance of the Milky Way. Fleecy cloud forms may also be projected on this cyclorama and made to drift across it.

So much for the sky.

Almost all his plays are "hands-on" in this way; they reveal an explicit attention to staging, characterization, lighting, music, and setting and include detailed descriptions of each. The prologue to *Camino Real* calls for "pounding surf or distant shellfire ... a number of glass-topped white iron tables and chairs ... a phoenix painted on silk ... and the [sign] 'Ritz Men Only'." Williams even specifies how the characters must appear, what music must haunt the background, how the characters should behave (including mannerisms like the way Alma Winemiller in *Summer and Smoke* should hold her hands cupped as though "receiving the wafer at Holy Communion," and the intent of the inflection and the facial expressions the characters should employ. (571) In these details, he reveals an exactness and care of craftsmanship, perhaps evincing a need to control his work, the principal aspect of his life in which he seems to have achieved some measure of freedom.

SYMBOLISM

Williams' use of symbols can create a depth to his plays that is practically unique among playwrights of his time. For example, Laura Wingfield's glass menagerie mirrors her personality: it is fragile, must be taken care of, and illustrates a desire to remain in the magical world of childhood. When Laura's high school crush, Jim O'Connor, persuades her to dance with him, he jostles the table and the horn of Laura's favorite animal, the unicorn, is broken. In a larger sense, the menagerie represents Tom's frustration with enclosure, with his inability to escape his home in light of the fact that he is held in check by so much innocent vulnerability. His abandonment of innocence and vulnerability is at the heart of the tragedy of his departure. Williams himself reveals, in *Where I Live*, that this symbolism is not accidental; rather, he contends, symbolism is a *process*, one that does not invariably lead to clarity:

> A play that is more of a dramatic poem than a play is bound to rest on metaphorical ways of expression. Symbols and their meanings must be arrived at through a period of time which is often a long one, requiring much patience, but if you wait out this period of time, if you permit it to clear as naturally as a sky after a storm, it will reward you, finally, with a puzzle which is still puzzling but which, whether you fathom it or not, still has the beautifully disturbing sense of truth, as much of that ambiguous quality as we are permitted to know in all our seasons and travels and places of short stay on this risky planet. (146)

But the pattern extends to the naming of his characters—Chance Wayne, Heavenly, Valentine Xavier, Rosario, Flora Goforth, Violet Venable, "Maggie the Cat." Blanche DuBois is no exception; appearing in white behind a paper lantern, Blanche (French for *white*) is compared to a moth. Characters thus become almost allegorical figures, which may well have been Williams' intention. Leonard Quirino notes in Clive Bloom's *American Drama* that:

> Williams has consistently (albeit with varying degrees of success) employed symbolism and the mythic mode to universalize the significance of the realistic action he posits, not only, apparently, because he thinks of symbolism and universality as essentials of art, but also because these qualities seem to be characteristic of his personal reactions to life in general. (95)

Whether aiming to universalize or not, Williams rarely used symbols in a subtle way; if he felt that a certain quality of character needed to be underscored, he did not hesitate to do so. To use symbols was for Williams to achieve a higher form of communication even than poetry: "[S]ymbols," he wrote in *Where I Live*, "when used respectfully, are the purest form of language." (66) Nevertheless, many critics have disapproved of or even derided Williams' use of symbolism—Quirino alludes to this—as clumsy or heavy-handed, and one has to wonder what Williams means by "respectful" use.

However, there are times when Williams' use of representative figures in his plays become too overt and thereby less effective. In the last scene of *The Night of the Iguana*, the symbolism between the iguana tied up under the house and the trapped feelings of the characters is directly explained in the dialogue between Hannah and Shannon:

> SHANNON: Iguana's have been known to bite their tails off when they're tied up by their tails.
>
> HANNAH: This one is tied up by its throat. It can't bite its own head off to escape from the end of the rope, Mr. Shannon. Can you look at me and tell me truthfully that you don't know it's able to feel pain and panic?
>
> SHANNON: You mean it's one of god's creatures?
>
> HANNAH: If you want to put it that way, yes, it is. Mr. Shannon, will you please cut it loose, set it free? Because if you don't, I will.
>
> SHANNON: Can you look at me and tell me truthfully that this reptilian creature, tied up down there, doesn't mostly disturb you because of its parallel situation to your Grampa's dying-out effort to finish one last poem, Miss Jelkes? (III)

In case the audience is unsure of the significance, it is immediately clear after old Nonno makes his first coherent speech after finishing the poem, and when Shannon and Maxine, the owners of the tourist homes, decide to stay as two lonely creatures bound together; and when Grampa dies just before the curtain closes. Williams clearly ties up all "loose ends" quickly.

Perhaps one of the most heavy-handed uses of symbolism is in *The Rose Tattoo*. In this play, Serafina, an older Italian woman, is rendered almost insane by the loss of her beloved husband, Rosario. Their daughter, Rose, is trying to escape the confines of the dressmaker's house where they live. Throughout the play, real roses and the color rose are referenced to stand for many things: love, the decaying of love, the passage of time, infidelity, and desire. When the play opens, Serafina delle Rose sits waiting for her husband to return, a bowl of roses on the dining room table. She has a rose in her hair, and wears a dress of rose silk, and holds a yellow paper fan with a rose on it. The audience is told that on the night their daughter, Rosa, was conceived, a strange thing happened:

> SERAFINA: Senti! That night I woke up with a burning pain on me, here, on my left breast! A pain like a needle, quick, quick, hot little stitches. I turned on the light, I uncovered my breast!—On it I saw the rose tattoo of my husband!
> ASSUNTA: Rosario's tattoo?
> SERAFINA: I screamed. But when he woke up, it was gone. It only lasted a moment. But I did see it, and I did know, when I saw it, that I had conceived, that in my body another rose was growing! (I)

Elsewhere in this play other references to roses abound. Rosario's lover comes in to request a man's shirt be sewn from a "piece of rose-colored silk which she holds up like a banner"; Serafina describes Rosario as having "hair on his head as thick and black as mine is and skin on him smooth and sweet as a yellow rose petal"; Rosa's suitor, Jack, brings roses when he comes to meet Serafina; Serafina calls her husband "a rose of a man" and explains that whenever he came home she "sometimes even ... put a rose in my hair!" Alavaro, Serafina's suitor, wears rose oil on his head, and sports the eponymous rose tattoo on his chest. When he later grabs Serafina up in a passionate embrace, he exclaims: "No, no, I know—I know that what warms the world, that is what makes it summer! Without it, the rose—the rose would not grow on the bush; the fruit would not grown on the tree!" And finally, Jack, Rose's boyfriend, tells her that she sees him "through—rose-colored—glasses." This very full use of rose imagery is often said to detract from scenes that begin as melodramatic; but one suspects that Williams knew of the effect his experiment would produce.

CRITICISM

In the early part of his career, Williams received the Pulitzer Prize for *A Streetcar Named Desire* and *Cat on a Hot Tin Roof* and the New York Drama Critics' Circle Award for *The Glass Menagerie, A Streetcar Named*

Desire, Cat on a Hot Tin Roof, and *The Night of the Iguana.* It might be that the landslide fame of his first few plays contributed to the rapid diminution of his reputation as "the greatest living playwright in the English-speaking world" when he changed his style.

Because Williams revisited his themes in his later plays, some critics claimed he was simply recycling earlier work, without ever moving beyond it. (Given the intimacy between Williams' life and his work, though, and the course of his life, this is only to be expected.) Worse, they said the plays were becoming more melodramatic and had lost their early lyrical realism—that they were now just ridiculous. Critics further opined that his characters were too similar to those of his early work; his mothers remained suffocating figures, his protagonists lost souls, and his women sexually repressed. In short, it was felt that Williams' later plays read like parodies of his earlier work—melodramatic, with overwrought dialogue, typical situations, two-dimensional characters, and predictable plots. These later plays were faulted too for using sex, violence, and the grotesque to attract audiences through sensationalism. Williams was trapped—for the more he wrote, the more he repeated himself, and the more he repeated himself the more he *wanted* to write.

But Williams found the act of writing to be less a release than an obsession so integral to his identity that, despite both his critical decline and the new pain of rehashing old pain, he could not put it aside. His friend Gore Vidal, in "Some Memories of the Glorious Bird and an Earlier Self," summarized the apparent stagnation of Williams' writing:

> Williams is the sort of writer who does not develop; he simply continues. By the time he was an adolescent he had his themes. Constantly, he plays and replays the small but brilliant set of cards. I am not aware that any new information (or feeling?) has got through to him in the twenty-eight years since our Roman Spring. (974)

Williams' memoirs show his acute awareness of the critical reception he received—criticism that was often venomous. Mostly, audiences and critics alike faulted him for being less and less capable of creating prose that communicated the human experience with the moving force of *Cat* or *Streetcar.*

It may be that his dependency drugs and alcohol, which grew with his career, contributed to his lack of focus. Even from the very start of his writing career, one sees the presence of alcohol as an escape in almost every work. Many of his characters confront some form of addiction: Blanche DuBois sneaks nips from a whiskey bottle, Princess in *Sweet Bird of Youth* needs her hashish; Shannon in *The Night of the Iguana* fights alcoholism. And Williams was not unaware of the public's perception of him as a degenerate drug user whose personal problems were destroying his work. He recognizes in *Memoirs* that, although his work in the theater sometimes brought him out of his stupor in the 1960s, all these productions were "disastrous—due to my inability to cope with the preparations of them and with a turn, in my work, toward a new style and a new creative world with which the reviewers and the audiences found it very hard to empathize so abruptly." (207) Truly, Williams seemed powerless to separate his work from his psyche, even when he was able to recognize the problematic nature of the connection. Friends saw this, too. Elia Kazan explains in *The Kindness of Strangers* that "Everything in [Williams'] life is in his plays, and everything in his plays is in his life." (179) Escapism is ubiquitous in both.

Critics also attacked Williams' later plays as being too pretentious, loosely philosophical, or derivative of acknowledged experimental playwrights like Beckett, Albee, and Pinter. Saddick explains that many felt Williams was "so exhausted from his indulgences with drugs and alcohol that he was unable to think coherently, or that in his twilight years he must be running out of ideas for new plays and was therefore desperately and pathetically trying to imitate the popular avant-garde drama of his younger contemporaries." (149) Stein, however, understands the change in Williams' work as a reflection of a change in the motivation of it:

> Theatrical and engaging plays like *Cat on a Hot Tin Roof* and *Sweet Bird of Youth* gave way to small-scaled, experimental chamber plays like *Gnadiges Fraulein*, *In the Bar of a Tokyo Hotel*, *Small Craft Warnings*, and *Out Cry*. Consumed by his own neuroses, Williams wrote these decidedly unpopular plays as forms of self-analysis, and the exorcism through his art was more important to him than the courting of public favor. (5)

In other words, Williams' writing had become even more autobiographical and egocentric; he was paying more attention to the needs his writing fulfilled and less to what audiences wanted. The result was work that may not have been suited to the consumption of his particular public.

Others argue that Williams' popularity declined simply because he abandoned a specific stylistic aspect of his earlier plays: the precarious balance between fantasy and reality. Beginning with *Camino Real*, Williams abandoned conventional technique and took more experimental approaches, and according to Saddick these plays "were not entertaining enough in terms of the expectations that go along with the 'sensitive realism' typical of Williams' earlier Broadway successes." (132) Supporters of Williams' work have always believed that Williams was attempting to keep pace with the *avant-garde* works of his contemporaries; but it is only recently that others have seen Williams' later plays in a positive light. Saddick extends her assertion that Williams was a victim of the theater market:

> The expectations of the popular press in this country, however, prevented them from accepting Williams' departure from the traditional, more commercial plays presented on Broadway ... which often only flirted with anti-realistic devices, to the minimalist exploration of language, character, and action that challenged realistic presentation altogether. (12)

Another point of dissention among critics is Williams' portrayal of women. Most agree that the earlier female characters have greater depth and emotional resonance than do characterizations by other playwrights of his genre. There is a division, though, between those who believe Williams was sympathetic to his female characters and those who see him as an acknowledged or unacknowledged misogynist. For example, Stanley Kowalski's rape of his sister-in-law in *Streetcar* can be read as justified by the text: Blanche, flouting the efforts of the aggressively working-class Stanley with her affected mannerisms and obvious distaste for the squalor of Elysian Fields, can be seen as deserving comeuppance and the rape as a way to force her to face reality. But Lant claims in "A Streetcar Named Misogyny" that Williams' misogyny, if it exists, is not of his own making:

[t]he misogyny is not peculiar to Williams but exists in his work as a reflection of society (and its attitudes toward women) to which he belongs. In this light, we can understand why *Streetcar* expresses a great compassion and affection for Blanche (a humane response to the suffering of woman, a respectful acknowledgement of her humanity) and at the same time an intense hostility and prejudice toward her (a misogynist response to her very femaleness and to her vulnerability to rape, a reduction of Blanche to the status of metaphor, bearer of meaning rather than creator of meaning). (3–4)

It is fair to say that Williams not only knows these women but also identifies with them. He is sympathetic; he said that Blanche DuBois was a reflection of himself, and his other women can easily be believed, by extension, also to reflect his frailties.

Williams remains an object of fascination for both critics and audiences. Truly, the exploration of his life and works here is cursory—there are many other recurrent themes and character types that demand a more in-depth explication. But one thing remains clear: all of Williams' characters are sensitive people struggling against their situations to the best of their abilities. They pursue a better life, hoping, as Williams seems to have hoped, to find peace elsewhere.

Like his characters, Williams fled reality. He skipped the openings of his plays, retreating instead to Acapulco, or Rome, or London. His lovers were numerous, and, with the exception of Frank Merlo, they were temporary distractions. Always in search of the next distraction, he tried through alcohol and drug abuse to escape the next play or place or person. But even during his least coherent days, when his drug abuse left him unable to walk reliably, he continued to write with a feverish dedication. The writing was an attempt to redeem himself, to free himself from the morass his life had become; but most importantly, it was something that he *needed* to do. Pursued by demons of his own making, he could hardly escape, and writing, the creation of character and situation, was a way to face his various selves. For he *had* to face them: as Tom Wingfield's final speech in *The Glass Menagerie* implies, Williams was well aware of the consequences of fleeing one's ghosts:

I traveled around a great deal. The cities swept about me like dead leaves, leaves that were brightly colored but torn away from the branches. I would have stopped, but I was pursued by something. It always came upon me unawares, taking me altogether by surprise. Perhaps it was a familiar bit of music. Perhaps it was only a piece of transparent glass. Perhaps I am walking along a street at night, in some strange city, before I have found companions. I pass the lighted window of a shop where perfume is sold. The window is filled with pieces of colored glass, tiny transparent bottles in delicate colors, like bits of a shattered rainbow. Then all at once my sister touches my shoulder. I turn around and look in her eyes. Oh, Laura, Laura, I tried to leave you behind me, but I am more faithful than I intended to be! I reach for a cigarette, I cross the street, I run into the movies or a bar, I buy a drink, I speak to the nearest stranger—anything that can blow your candles out!

Williams recognized his faults, both as a writer and as a man. As he testifies in *Where I Live* (171), it was through the writing that he tried create from the tangle of his circumstances some semblance of order:

And so I presume to insist there must be somewhere truth to be pursued each day with words that are misunderstood and feared because they are the words of an Artist, which must always remain a word most compatible with the word Revolutionary, and so be more than a word. Therefore, from youth into age I have continued and will still continue the belief and the seeking, until that time when time can no longer concern me.

Works Cited

Adler, Thomas P. "Tennessee Williams's 'Personal Lyricism': Toward an Androgynous Form." *Realism and the American Dramatic Tradition*, ed. William W. Demastes. Tuscaloosa: University of Alabama, 1996.

Bloom, Clive, ed. *American Drama*. New York: St. Martin's, 1995.

Bloom, Harold, ed. *Tennessee Williams*. Modern Critical Interpretations. New York: Chelsea House, 2000.

Boxill, Roger. *Tennessee Williams*. Modern Dramatists. London: Palgrave Macmillan, 1989.

Cohn, Ruby. *Dialogue in American Drama*. Bloomington: Indiana University Press, 1971.

Day, Christine R., and Bob Woods, eds. *Where I Live: Selected Essays by Tennessee Williams*. New York: New Directions, 1978.

Devlin, Albert J. *Conversations with Tennessee Williams*. Jackson: University Press of Mississippi, 1986.

———, and Nancy Tischler, eds. *The Selected Letters of Tennessee Williams*. Vol. 1. Sewanee: The University of the South, 2000.

Donahue, Francis. *The Dramatic World of Tennessee Williams*. New York: Frederick Ungar, 1964.

Falk, Signi Lenea. *Tennessee Williams*. New Haven: College and University Press, 1961.

Fedder, Norman J. *The Influence of D.H. Lawrence on Tennessee Williams*. The Hague: Mouton, 1966.

Lant, Kathleen Margaret. "A Streetcar Named Misogyny." *Violence in Drama*, ed. James Redmond. Cambridge: Cambridge University Press, 1991.

Leavitt, Richard F., ed. *The World of Tennessee Williams*. New York: G.P. Putnam's Sons, 1978.

Leverich, Lyle. *Tom: The Unknown Tennessee Williams*. New York: Crown, 1995.

Nelson, Benjamin. *Tennessee Williams: The Man and His Work*. New York: Ivan Obelensky, 1961.

Pagan, Nicholas. *Rethinking Literary Biography: A Postmodern Approach to Tennessee Williams*. London and Toronto: Associated University Presses, 1993.

Robinson, Marc. *The Other American Drama*. New York: Cambridge University Press, 1994.

Saddick, Annette J. *The Politics of Reputation: The Critical Reception of Tennessee Williams' Later Plays*. London: Associated University Presses, 1999.

Sarote, Georges-Michael. "Fluidity and Differentiation in Three Plays by Tennessee Williams: *The Glass Menagerie, A Streetcar Named Desire*, and *Cat on a Hot Tin Roof*." *Staging Difference: Cultural Pluralism in American Theater and Drama*, ed. Marc Maufort. New York: Peter Lang, 1995.

Savran, David. *Communists, Cowboys, and Queers: The Politics of Masculinity in the Works of Arthur Miller and Tennessee Williams*. Minneapolis: University of Minnesota, 1992.

Spoto, Donald. *The Kindness of Strangers: The Life of Tennessee Williams*. Boston: Little, Brown, 1985.

Stein, Roger B. "*The Glass Menagerie* Revisited: Catastrophe Without Violence." *Tennessee Williams's* The Glass Menagerie. Modern Critical Interpretations, ed. Harold Bloom. New York: Chelsea House Publishers, 1988.

Tischler, Nancy M. *Tennessee Williams: Rebellious Puritan*. New York: Putnam, 1963.

Tharpe, Jack, ed. *Tennessee Williams: 13 Essays*. Jackson: University Press of Mississippi, 1980.

Vidal, Gore. "Some Memories of the Glorious Bird and an Earlier Self." *The New York Review of Books* (Feb. 5, 1976).

Williams, Dakin, and Shepherd Mead. *Tennessee Williams: An Intimate Biography*. New York: Arbor House, 1983.

Williams, Tennessee. "Creator of *The Glass Menagerie* Pays Tribute to Laurette Taylor." *The New York Times* (Dec. 5, 1949).

———. *Memoirs*. Garden City, NY: Doubleday, 1975.

———. *Tennessee Williams: Plays 1937–1955*, eds. Kenneth Holdich and Mel Gussow. New York: Library of America, 2000.

———. *Tennessee Williams: Plays 1957–1980*, eds. Mel Gussow and Kenneth Holdich. New York: New Directions Publishing, 2000.

Windham, Donald. *Lost Friendships: A Memoir of Truman Capote, Tennessee Williams, and Others*. New York: Morrow, 1987.

NANCY M. TISCHLER

Romantic Textures in Tennessee Williams's Plays and Short Stories

I believe in Michelangelo, Velásquez and Rembrandt; in the might of design, the mystery of color, the redemption of all things by beauty everlasting and the message of art that has made these hands blessed. Amen.

This, Tennessee Williams proclaimed to be his own creed as an artist.[1] Like his "Poet" of the short story by that name, Tennessee Williams was a natural romantic whose very existence was one of "benevolent anarchy" ("The Poet," 246). His artistic *creed* (a term of some significance to a man nurtured in theology) signals the primacy of the artist, not God. He was dedicated to: (1) the power of "design" or artistic control over the material world; (2) the "mystery" of color or the non-rational, supernatural gift of beauty, affecting the artist and the audience; (3) the "redemption" of all things by "beauty"—an act of salvation by means of created and experienced splendor; (4) the "message" of art, the need to communicate the artist's vision of reality to the audience; and (5) the "blessedness" of his hands—his conviction that he is the chosen vessel for this important work.

From *The Cambridge Companion to Tennessee Williams.* © 1997 by Cambridge University Press. Reprinted by permission.

CREDO: "I BELIEVE IN..." WILLIAMS'S
ROMANTIC INFLUENCES

Thomas Lanier Williams, also known as Tennessee, was born to be a visionary. He gathered ideas, images, themes, and phrases as he wandered through life and wove colorful romantic pictures onto the dark background of his increasing realism to form grand designs and vivid contrasts. He lived his life as a peripatetic poet, one of the everlasting company of fugitives who discover their vocation in their art, transforming experience and giving shape to visions.[2]

Descended from colonial settlers and pioneers, he was quintessentially American, but never a typical pragmatic middle American. He saw himself as the archetypal outsider: a poet in a practical world, a homosexual in a heterosexual society. Living in the "Century of Progress," he preferred candlelight to electricity. A Southerner who lamented the loss of a dignity, elegance, and sense of honor, he was never satisfied with the dreary present and its flat speech. Williams yearned for "long distance," for "cloudy symbols of high romance," or what romantics called the "yonder bank."[3] His characters love a lost, idealized past ("Blue Mountain"), and they live for a dangerous, problematic future ("Terra Incognita"). From beginning to end, Williams's theatrical struggle was also a romantic quest for Parnassus. It was romantic dreamers—quixotic and tattered old warriors, fragile young poets, frightened misfits—whom he celebrated in his poems, stories, novels, and plays. Romanticism was the very fabric of his life and work woven throughout. In his early self-descriptions for Audrey Wood, his longtime agent, he presented a persona deliberately crafted as the romantic loner.[4] This portrait of the peripatetic, penniless writer was then polished and repeated in many articles, interviews, and biographies which followed. (Note especially Conversations with Tennessee Williams[5] and Where I Live.)

In a statement for the press, developed at the time The Night of the Iguana was premiering in New York, he showed that he was aware of his obsession with what he called "the Visionary Company": "This new play, The Night of the Iguana, and the one to follow, off-Broadway, which is presently titled The Milk Train Doesn't Stop Here Anymore," he explained, "both contain major characters who are poets, and this was not planned, it just happened." He then continues: "In Suddenly Last Summer the chief topic of discussion and violent contention was also a poet. So obviously the archetype of the poet has become an obsessive figure, a leit-motif in my recent work for the stage, and possibly was always, since Tom Wingfield in *The Glass Menagerie* was a poet, too, and so was Val Xavier in *Orpheus Descending* essentially a poet, for a singer is a kind of poet, too, just as a poet is a kind of singer."

He then explains that "the idea, the image, of a poet has come to represent to me, as a writer, an element in human-life that put up the strongest resistance to that which is false and impure, in himself and the world..." Such a person is "always a tragic antagonist."

Finally, waxing eloquent about this figure, Williams announces that, "If he is really a poet, by vocation, not affectation, his sword Excalibur or his Holy Grail, is truth as he himself conceives it, and he believes in it as an absolute, as many non-practicing poets in the world also do."[6] Here, most clearly we have the romantic imagery of the chosen vessel for divinely inspired activity.

Williams's letters, his early drafts, his short stories, and his plays often signal the particular artists whose lives captured his attention: D. H. Lawrence, Vachel Lindsay, William Wordsworth, and George Gordon, Lord Byron in the early days; F. Scott Fitzgerald, Mishima Yukio, Jane Bowles, and Jackson Pollock later on; and Hart Crane always.

This whole inclination to observe the world and its people through the eyes of the romantic came as naturally to Williams as writing did. He was related to both Sidney Lanier, the nineteenth-century poet, and to John Sharp Williams, one of the more eloquent of the Southern political orators.[7] To have spent his early youth in the Mississippi Delta, in the home of an Episcopal minister, in the midst of people speaking rich Southern dialects, would be adequate to establish his taste for purple prose and romantic thoughts. It also fixed his identification of youth, Eden innocence, and the bucolic South.

He spent many hours of his childhood in the well-stocked library of his grandfather, a classically educated man. (A portion of this library is currently held in the Tennessee Williams Collection at Washington University in St. Louis.) Among the earliest reading for the young boy were "The Lady of Shalott" and the novels of Sir Walter Scott, the poetry of Coleridge and Poe. Tom Williams's early flowery style derived originally from this saturation in such lyric poets as Sara Teasdale and Edna St. Vincent Millay. In the "Frivolous Version" of a "Preface to My

Poems," he noted that he "began writing verse at about the time of puberty," and that his earliest success was an "apostrophe to death" which named a number of the lyric women poets, ending with a tribute to "glorious Millay."[8]

In *Summer and Smoke*, Williams parodies these memories of his adolescent self and his fellow poets of the women's club, portraying the typical genteel Southern poetry club gathering in the manse for lemonade and uplift. The scene reflects Williams's changing preferences among romantic poets. Miss Alma, like her creator, finds the atmosphere of the gathering vaguely oppressive. Her selection of the "dangerous" poet—William Blake—for her topic, foreshadows her sexual rebellion. Without fully realizing that Blake's vision violates her tidy Puritan world, she is drawn to his lyrics because they speak to her own love and frustration. (In another scene, she quotes Oscar Wilde, before she realizes her embarrassing source.) Blake does hold the key to the hidden tiger lurking almost out of sight in the forest of Miss Alma's nature.[9] The short story out of which this play grew, "The Yellow Bird," is even clearer in its rejection of rigid Puritanism. For Williams, it became clear that the art he cherishes is rude, violent, outrageous. He believed he was called to live and think like Cassandra (in *Battle of Angels*), his early social rebel and Val Xavier, his vagrant sensualist.

Tennessee Williams believed that he could never discover his own richest potential until he rejected the anemic romanticism of his repressive, conformist home for the full-bodied romantic life of *Sturm und Drang*. In the months prior to college in 1929, he immersed himself in the biography of "Mad Shelley" and was, as Lyle Leverich tells us, "fascinated that the poet had been wild, passionate and dissolute" (99). His first escape from home came with his enrollment at the University of Missouri at Columbia, where he had a taste of independence. There, as a journalism major, he expanded his understanding of the literary romantics. We know that he read and wrote extensively, finding himself drawn to the nineteenth-century French and Russian writers.

While at Missouri, in 1930, he wrote *Beauty Is the Word* for Professor Ramsay's one-act play contest. Lyle Leverich, in *Tom: The Unknown Tennessee*,[10] notes that the play is significant "not only because its Shelleyan fervor reflects Tom's own enthusiasm for the poet but also because the theme, while not a restatement of Shelley's atheism, was Tom's first attack upon the inhibitions of Puritanism and its persecution of the artist..." In short, he was depicting "the heroism of the freethinker" (113). In a stirring speech, the heroine announces: "Fear is ugliness. God—at least *my* God—is Beauty" (Leverich, 113). Going even beyond Keats's Grecian Urn, by proclaiming that beauty is God, Williams aligned himself with the aesthetes.

The sudden conclusion to his studies at the University of Missouri in 1932, when his father angrily brought him home and put him to work in the shoe factory, reinforced his hatred of St. Louis, factories, and the industrialized world of work. The years 1932 to 1935 were a nightmare for him, the basis for numerous of his later stories and plays about life trapped in a stultifying home situation and a dead-end job. These years fixed permanently in his psyche his recurring themes of claustrophobia and the hunger for "romance." From this torturous time, he forged his image of the Poet climbing out of the factory to the roof, where he can see the sky, the stars, and the distant world. This autobiographical image, which appeared in the early play *Stairs to the Roof*, was to find its richest expression in *The Glass Menagerie*.

Working among intellectual strangers, living at home in the midst of constant hostility also reinforced his sense of loneliness. A decade later, he wrote to Audrey Wood, "Sometimes the solitary struggle of writing is almost too solitary for endurance!"[11] For him, writing was not a pleasant pastime, but an emotional hunger. It was this life of quiet desperation that demanded "redemption" by "beauty everlasting."

It was in 1936, having begun evening classes at Washington University in St. Louis, that he found companions in his quest. At the university, he was an active member of the College Poetry Society, with Clark Mills and William Jay Smith, two poets who were also dedicated to the literary life.

In addition, he found the Mummers, a small theatre group in St. Louis that provided him both company and left-wing orthodoxy typical of the thirties. Working with them, he had some of his earliest—if ephemeral—theatrical successes (*Candles to the* Sun and *The Fugitive Kind*,[12] as well as an anti-war curtainraiser for Irwin Shaw's play *Bury the Dead*, were his main contributions).

At Washington University Williams was also continuing his reading and thinking about the English romantics. There, from the distinguished Professor Otto Heller, he must have learned something of the Germanic philosophic background of the romantic movement, which Coleridge especially had found useful in the development and explication of his ideas.

Though he did frequently quote both Wordsworth and Coleridge, Williams had a pronounced inclination toward the second wave of English romantics. To have preferred not only the poetry, but also the morality of Byron, Keats, and Shelley to the more conservative Wordsworth and Coleridge would have been considered an act of rebellion at the time. (Irving Babbitt, in his famous book on Rousseau, had condemned the younger romantics as "diseased.") Others agreed that their ideas were dangerous, their lives depraved. Byron had boasted publicly (and outrageously) of having slept with two hundred women in two years. Shelley was a wife-swapper who founded a free-love colony.[13] In his twenties and beyond, Williams came to accept the romantics' rejection of "obsolete standards of family life and morality." Such celebrations of the "Cavalier" spirit delighted this rebellious puritan.

The young Tom Williams explored the bohemian world in college (after Washington University, a year at the University of Iowa, where he majored in theatre), and later in New Orleans. In 1939, having finally graduated from college, he left home for good, though he was never entirely free of the cords of love, need, and duty that continually drew him back. The young writer joined the company of fellow bohemians in New Orleans. (Later he spoke affectionately of the cities in America which were home to artists, noting Key West and San Francisco as meccas for writers and painters.[14]) There, trading his old image of the choirboy lyric writer for his new persona as the vagabond poet, Williams changed his nom de plume to "Tennessee."

In these early days, Hart Crane became his mythic hero. In the character and poetry of this modern American romantic he found a perfect mirror for his own experience:[15] the poet on the wing, hungry for the deepest experiences of life, in love with beauty and with poetry, seeking to express the ineffable. Additionally, in the outcast D. H. Lawrence, he found echoes of his own passions. (He visited Lawrence's widow, Frieda, and wrote a play about Lawrence, "I Rise in Flame, Cried the Phoenix," which pictures his unquenchable spirit.) Such latter-day romantics appealed to his faith in his art and his image of the poet as the outsider. They also helped him to define his own experience, give form to his very real passions.

Decades later, having embraced the "Bitch Goddess Success," he found he was increasingly disgusted with himself and his world. He explored authors who had always interested him and who gave voice to his disillusionment: Proust, Baudelaire, and Rimbaud—French neo-romantic symbolists.[16] Plays such as *The Night of the Iguana*, *Suddenly Last Summer*, or *Sweet Bird of Youth* have clear ties to these artists. His defrocked priest, decadent poet, and obsolescent artist are painful reminders of the fierce romantics he had celebrated earlier. Far more decadent than the English romantics, these *fin de siècle* French writers mirrored Williams's own declivity. Rimbaud, a recent critic commented, was noted for: "Furiously hallucinogenic imagery (fueled by hashish and absinthe), bourgeoisie-skewering rudeness, mysticism, proud bisexuality and an adolescent taste for despair."[17] By 1969, Williams himself had sunk into the world of drugs, writing fragments of stories that tended toward fantasy. This trend was foreshadowed as early as the 1948 story of "The Poet," when the vat of mysterious fermented drink fuels the poet's ecstasies and the young followers' orgiastic celebration (246).

Williams's influences became increasingly eclectic. In love with the exotic, he was enamored of Eastern mysticism and Asian dramatic forms. This astonished Williams's fans when they saw *The Milk Train Doesn't Stop Here Anymore*, with Flora dressed in a ceremonial Kabuki costume and the final spotlight on the Angel of Death's mysteriously lighted mobile. The Japanese writer Mishima Yukio was a friend and an especially important influence.[18] He and Williams first met in the sixties, discovered they shared a publisher and tastes in life and art; they considered themselves soul mates. In 1970, Williams traveled to Asia, visiting with Mishima (though not with his traditional family in his home) and saw him shortly before his suicide.[19]

Other neo-romantics, like William Butler Yeats, added to Tennessee Williams's allusions, his worldview, and his imagery. He was an aesthetically adventurous writer who read voraciously and traveled constantly, exploring many regions and ideas. Even those he chose to designate or quote are by no means the only ones who inspired him. To the very end of his life, he was insatiable—reading the latest books, seeing the new plays, experimenting with new styles. Some of his most experimental pieces are yet to be published. Tennessee Williams's early love of romantic poetry was to leave a deep mark on his plays and stories: poetic speech became his signature. Critics were regularly impressed by the lyricism of his drama.

These "Blessed Hands":
Williams as an Inspired Writer

> The poet distilled his own liquor and had become so
> accomplished in this art that he could produce a fermented
> drink from almost any kind of organic matter. He carried it
> in a flask strapped about his waist, and whenever fatigue
> overtook him he would stop at some lonely point and raise
> the flask to his lips. Then the world would change color as a
> soap bubble penetrated by a ray of light and a great vitality
> would surge and break as a limitless ocean through him. The
> usual superfluity of the impressions would fall away so that
> his senses would combine in a single vast ray of perception
> which blinded him to lesser phenomena and experience as
> candles might be eclipsed in a chamber of glass exposed to a
> cloudless meridian of the sun. ("The Poet," 746)

This visionary poet's experience parallels Wordsworth's "spots of time"
in "The Prelude." In this extended autobiographical poem, Wordsworth
also described himself as "the Poet." He thought that his writing was
"emotion recollected in tranquillity"—an idea Williams frequently
quoted and occasionally experienced. As he said, his writing was rarely a
result of tranquil recollection. He was far more inclined to the
"spontaneous overflow of powerful feeling." In any case, inspiration is
essential to the true romantic. Although Williams used real details of his
individual experience and dreams, he could not create without this
mysterious gift from the muses. This explains Williams's assertion that
writing was a *vocation* for him. He had no choice, as his biography clearly
demonstrates. During his prolonged apprenticeship in writing, he
borrowed, begged, and sponged off friends and family; he signed on for
one subsistence-level job after another, rarely holding any for more than
a few months—long enough to allow him to survive. Any other work
seemed irrelevant in the face of this calling to be a writer. Even writing
for the films, in 1943, when he spent six months with MGM, was too
artificial and claustrophobic for this free spirit.

    Perhaps as a result of spending his first years intimately connected
with the Episcopal Church, hearing the language of spiritual leadership,

he believed that poetry was a high calling. Over and over, he said that "work" was his favorite four-letter word. It was certainly central to his concept of integrity. He thought no sexual or contractual violation so corrupt as the betrayal of his art or the abandonment of his writing.

Like Coleridge, Tennessee Williams sensed this power of inspiration rushing through him. His references to the wind and his love of wind chimes[20] blend romantic with Pentecostal wind imagery. (Consider "Ode to the West Wind" and "Aeolian Harp" as romantic precedents). When this inspiration faltered, he followed the path of Hart Crane, Coleridge, and de Quincey, using sex, drugs, and alcohol to induce an artificial ecstasy.

Tennessee Williams was a latter-day incarnation of Plato's Poet-as-Inspired-Madman. Biographies and character sketches note the artist writing with a frenzy that astonished visitors. He laughingly said he was not a writer but a compulsive typist. His letters testify to his demonic attack on typewriters, which frequently broke under his constant pounding. Landladies were reluctant to disturb the piles of crumpled paper they found littering the floor where he worked. Scholars find themselves puzzling at the various pages on different papers, unnumbered, often written on different machines.[21] He could work on several pieces at a time, blending in his fertile imagination bits of experience, remembered poetry, phrases he had heard on the street, and images from his reading. Like Coleridge, as described in *The Road to Xanadu* (by John Livingston Lowes), Williams read widely, especially when considering writing about actual people. For example, when working on the life of Lindsay, he read E. L. Masters's life; he spent a long time reading about D. H. Lawrence for a long Lawrence play he finally abandoned. As a result of reading the latest books on Zelda Fitzgerald, which Andreas Brown, the owner of the Gotham Book Mart, had sent him along with other books, knowing of his interest in the Fitzgeralds and Hemingway, Williams was inspired to write *Clothes for a Summer Hotel*. But the magic moment of creativity came not in an intellectual mixing of notes into a coherent thesis, but in the powerful act of chemical fusion that took place in the "deep well" of the unconscious.

Also, in the mode of the true romantic spirit, he never considered a work completely finished. He would attend rehearsals, watch the movement, listen to the sound of the lines delivered on stage, and then revise whole sections, crossing out scenes, revising movement, adding dialogue. Many of his plays exist in variant editions; even when published, they were not complete—largely because they were not satisfactory copies of the Platonic image in his mind. ("The Yellow Bird," then *Summer and Smoke*, evolved into *The Eccentricities of a Nightingale*; *Battle of Angels* metamorphosed into *Orpheus Descending*; *Confessional* grew into *Small Craft Warnings*; and "Three Players of a Summer Game" became *Cat on a Hot Tin Roof*, which had at least two possible third acts.)

The real drive of the romantic is to give form to the individual God-given vision. Like most romantics, Tennessee Williams wrote most powerfully when he worked "inside out." Whether describing his own adventures as a young artist, his mother's pain, his sister's tragedy, or his father's incomprehension, Williams was at his best when his subject was the Dakin/Williams family. He knew that the written words always fell short of the noetic experience; thus his ideal poet avoided freezing his ideas by fixing them on paper, preferring to keep them fluid ("The Poet," 247). Later, he was able to expand this family circle to include theatre people and homeless wanderers, all of whom shared his own values and anguish.

Like the Wandering Jew or the Ancient Mariner, the Williams hero is the lonely stranger who bears a mark setting him apart from other men—a special hunger, an unsatisfied need. Handsome and cursed, he dominates the stage as he does the community. He is the sun to their moons of desire ("One Arm"). A non-conformist, he must speak his outrageous Truth, facing turmoil, expulsion, and death. The Poet (of the short story) is washed by the sea and bleached by the sun until he is finally free of the corrupting flesh.

Tennessee Williams, a child of the Church, born during Passion Week, readily commingled aesthetic and religious mysticism, eroding barriers between art and faith. His imagery of the Poet is frequently laced with references to Christ. Sometimes disciples, the "women," the Pharisees, the Sanhedrin, and the mob elaborate this Williams Christology. Variants on the Crucifixion are common in his work. At one point, when discussing *The Night of the Iguana* with Bob MacGregor, his editor at New Directions, he noted he had "Too many Christ-figures in my work, too cornily presented." He asked that MacGregor remove the extraneous one he had written into Shannon's first entrance description.[22]

Like the brooding Byron, Williams's Poet/Wanderer is a magnet to women. Whether he is the virile farmer in *Seven Descents of Myrtle* or the anguished defrocked preacher in *The Night of the Iguana*, this outcast hero marches to the beat of his own drummer. A creature of flesh, he attracts the lust of others, but needs more than the flesh for his satisfaction. Female characters too—Blanche and Alma—express this tormented dualism, hunger for sexual contact, subsequent self-loathing, and loneliness. They love poetry, cherish an impossible idealism, and despise their own physical needs.

The conflict of the spirit and the flesh is a central agony for the romantic artist: the act of creation is a mystical process of conception, pregnancy, and birth—an aesthetic Incarnation. As the Word was planted by God in the Virgin, so the Idea is the seed planted by Inspiration in the poet—e.g., Sebastian spent nine months nurturing each perfect poem. The eventual birth, after a fierce and painful time of labor, brings forth a creature separate from the bearer. It then takes on a public life of its own, over which the writer/parent has no control. The "incubus in his bosom" ("The Poet," 248) was both natural and invasive, demanding development regardless of the contrary will of the artist.

For Tennessee Williams, the "blessedness" of the artist is also his ironic source of damnation or torment. From the guitar-playing hobo of the Depression-era Delta to the contemporary All American, the Williams hero is unprotected by family, uncomfortable with companions. He inevitably draws hostility. Torn apart by dogs, blowtorched, castrated, or cannibalized, the Williams fugitive is finally chased to earth and destroyed in a catastrophic finale.

The Mystery of Color: The Romantic Portrayal of Reality

Transforming human experience into art, showing the complexity of human life on stage, was the ultimate challenge for Williams. Whether named Valentine Xavier, Kilroy, Chance Wayne, or Sebastian, the Williams mythic protagonist is a romanticized persona exploring and explaining facets of the artist himself. Williams acknowledged that he never developed a character who did not contain some quality of his own personality elaborated and developed for theatrical purposes.

Basing his dramas on his own anguished life, Tennessee Williams often portrayed the male/female attraction/conflict. The masculine/feminine identity, the need to individuate the growing personality, the love/hate conflicts of the family. Over time, he increasingly moved toward a more subtle symbolic use of multiple facets of human complexity. In *The Night of the Iguana*, for example, the virgin and the widow become spirit and flesh, as well as fully conceived characters. Shannon's good and bad angels demand he choose between two diametrically opposed visions of the future. The ending cannot be happy for him, for either choice demands the rejection of a part of his psyche.

An even more complex vision of the human psyche appears in *Out Cry* with the brother and sister, both of ambivalent gender, who appear to be two sides of a single person, the animus/anima. Williams acknowledges freely his belief in the dual nature of the artist, or at least his kind of romantic artist. Like Alma, Williams believed himself to be a double person, referring frequently to his "doppleganger" or his "blue devils," and to his double vision as "something cloudy, something clear."

In organic writing, the passionate manuscript grows naturally from the passionate life. Williams thereby felt justified in following Millay's caustic advice to burn his candle at both ends. He craved the intensely experienced moment, full of color, variety, and violence. Like Keats, he believed that he must "drink deep" in order to feel the full range of emotions. In himself and in others, Williams cherished the youthful sense of wonder that Keats characterized in "On First Looking into Chapman's Homer." Williams's central characters search for that "surprise" that leaves them "breathless upon a peak in Darien." Without this capacity for breaking out of his own body in the "rapture of vision," life is only another form of death.

In *Small Craft Warnings*, the young man from Iowa—an echo of the youthful Williams on his 1939 trip West—delights in his first view of the Pacific Ocean. The older scriptwriter—a reference to Williams in 1943 during his MGM period—sadly notes that he has lost that quality of amazement. The later works of Williams have the melancholy cast of the romantic who has outlived his childhood to become a sour stoic. The old doctor in *Small Craft Warnings*—painfully underscored by the playwright's brief appearance in the role himself—has lost even the ability to deliver the live child, much less to conceive one. In a sad letter he wrote to his friend and editor, Robert MacGregor from Key West in

1960, he said he was weary of writing but could not stop. "I am like old Aw Boo Ha, the tiger balm king of the Orient who kept building and building his palaces and gardens till they became grotesque because a fortune-teller told him that he would die when he stopped." *Small Craft Warnings, Moise and the World of Reason, Something Cloudy, Something Clear* all contain double or even triple images of the poet, the young man and the old, reflecting what Tennessee Williams called "corruption."

Over the years, as his idealism was tempered with reality, he learned to balance the lyricism with cynical descants, giving up his "early genius" for "the telling of marvelous stories" ("The Poet," 247). He found a mature voice in the subtle textures of human existence, the interplay of personalities, the "net" of words. He loved bold contrasts, startling climaxes, angry confrontations. In his delight with language, he indulged in the juxtaposition of romantic rhetoric with realistic put-down. When Blanche speaks of "Mr. Edgar Allan Poe," Stanley quotes Huey Long, a notorious Louisiana politician of the era. When Amanda refers to her skill in the "art of conversation," Tom laughingly acknowledges that she "sure can talk." Realism intrudes on the dreamer in the Williams drama, as it did in his life.

In a letter to Audrey Wood,[23] he clarified this trend for her and for himself. At the time, he was transforming *Battle of Angels* into *Orpheus Descending*. Apparently, Audrey, always a tough critic for her client/friend, did not have an immediately enthusiastic reaction. He tells her that he too was bothered by the earlier "juvenile poetics, the inflated style" and was seeking to "bring it down to earth," to give the character "a tougher, more realistic treatment." He notes that Cassandra was too "hi-faluting" in the original: "Behold Cassandra, shouting doom at the gates!" He notes that "all that sort of crap ... seemed so lovely to me in 1940. Unfortunately in 1940 I was younger and stronger and— curiously!—more confident writer than I am in the Fall of 1953. Now I am a maturer and more knowledgeable craftsman of the theatre, my experience inside and outside the profession is vastly wider..." But he still insists that some lyrical passages are justified by "heightened emotion." "It's only on rare occasions that our hearts are uncovered and their voices released and that's when poetry comes and the deepest emotion, and expression ... I think they should have this contrast to the coarse common speech. The coarseness is deliberate and serves a creative purpose which is not sensational." (He justified the use of

Kilroy in *Camino Real* in similar terms in a letter to Audrey Wood, February, 1946.) He concludes his long defense by insisting that, "Despite the coarse touches in the dialogue, I think the total effect of the play would be one of tragic purity..." This powerful letter reveals that Williams deliberately shifted levels of diction to match the dramatic flow of the play. He was a craftsman as well as a visionary.

The plot patterns of the plays reflect this romantic/realistic duality more effectively than do the stories and the other fiction. "Realistic" drama forced him to conform to recognizable, though exaggerated and compressed, human experience and dialogue. Even his dream visions have touches of reality when shaped for the stage. Short stories and novellas, by contrast, do not constrain the artist in the same way, freeing him to indulge his taste for magic realism. While Alma in *Summer and Smoke* is obliged to sit beneath the fountain's angel and pick up a traveling salesman, the more "magical" Alma in the short story of "The Yellow Bird" can bear a beautiful child who rides off on the back of a dolphin and returns with a cornucopia of treasure.

THE MESSAGE OF ART: COMMUNICATING WILLIAMS'S WORLD-VIEW

"We are all of us sentenced to solitary confinement in our own skins," says Val—and Tennessee. The barriers, walls, curtains in his plays signal the solitude of the individual and the difficulties of communication. Characters retreat to their cells only to meet briefly in bars or restaurants. Like Leibniz's monads, they are isolated, with minimal contact or insight.

The Poet, unable to bear this silence and solitude, is driven to communicate "the presence of something beyond the province of matter" ("The Poet," 251). Williams believed that writers are the messengers of transcendence, informing humanity that humdrum life behind the plow is not the full story. Poets help people to took towards heaven.

For Tennessee Williams, the world was the scene of epic battles—between the Flesh and the Spirit, Good and Evil, God and Satan, Gentle Jesus and Terrifying Jehovah. Unlike the more cynical post-Christian postmoderns, he insisted on the cyclorama as the background for his plays. A sweep of sky and sea, a rainforest; sounds of thunderstorms, lightning, and wind are all signals of God's sovereign power, dwarfing the human activities front and center in our consciousness. This brief moment on the stage of life is not the whole story; our choices here and now define humanity existentially.

In his multilayered creations, nothing is simple: the iguana is not just a small, ugly reptile; it represents mankind in the hands of an angry God. The turtles racing for the sea are not simply evidence of nature's prodigious wastefulness, they are symbols of humanity in the face of an avenging deity. For this child of the Church, each drama is a bit of symbolic action played out under the watchful eye of heaven. The youthful hours Tom Williams spent studying the stained glass windows of St. George's Episcopal Church in Clarksdale, Mississippi, reading the scripture passages, repeating the words of the services were not wasted. Although he rarely went into a church in his later years (even after his conversion to Catholicism in 1969) he did acknowledge that the mass at the local cathedral was more powerful drama than he could ever write. The historic bonds between the Church and the theatre were quite real to him.

Even the most bestial of people in the most superficial relationships feel the need to make connections, discovering moments of grace that are breathtaking. In *The Night of the Iguana*, Shannon and Hannah, who listen to the final lines of Nonno's sonnet have a magic moment of communication. In "The Mutilated," two old women in a seedy hotel room in the Vieux Carré discuss a vision of the Virgin and share a glass of Tokay wine and a Nabisco wafer. Such moments of grace are emanations of transcendence.

This three-storied universe gave Williams's work a remarkable range. In *Summer and Smoke*, he knew he was creating a medieval play with modern twists. In a letter to Audrey Wood he noted that it had a "... sort of Gothic quality—spiritually romantic—which I wanted to create. It is hard for you to use such stuff in a modern play for a modern audience, but I feel it is valid."[24]

Although both heaven and hell were part of his three-storied universe, they were romantic interpretations of the medieval cosmology. Echoing William Blake, Williams spoke of "Innocence" and "Experience" as polar opposites. He also saw that heaven was hell and hell was heaven in the topsy-turvy world of materialistic dreams. Sharing Wordsworth's concept of the innocent child ("Ode on

Intimations of Immortality") Tennessee Williams fully believed that he
had come into this world "trailing clouds of glory."

Like Wordsworth and Blake, he saw growing up as a process of
losing innocence and joy. His poetry and stories are full of images of free
children leaping over fences, gamboling in wild nature, drunk with
imagination and delight—like those who follow his "Poet." Childhood
for him was the halcyon age of Edenic wholeness. He was by nature a
follower of Rousseau. No Calvinist, he could not believe that the loss of
innocence was a result of sin. Rather it was the fault of society, which
refused to allow the child to remain free of fetters. Armies and factories
finally claimed the children, pulling them "home," safe from the song of
the Poet. Their voices were stilled.

Living in an era bombarded with the ideas of Freud, Williams
came to see the discovery of sexuality—the moment the child realized he
or she was naked—as the end of innocence. In *The Night of the Iguana*,
Shannon explains his own anger at his mother's furious interruption of
his childish masturbation. Her assertion that she spoke for God in her
unequivocal judgment was sufficient cause for the child to resent both
the parent and the deity.

In innocent love scenes like those in *The Rose Tattoo*, *Battle of
Angels*, and "A Field of Blue Children," Williams echoes Keats's
portrayal of the lovers caught in the moment of anticipation in the frieze
on the Grecian Urn or melting into delight in "The Eve of St. Agnes."
Following their natural inclinations, untroubled by the nasty-minded
puritan culture, the young lovers enjoy fully the prelapsarian spirit of joy
in sharing their bodies with one another.

This world and its people are doomed to final destruction. From
beginning to end, from *Battle of Angels* to *The Red Devil Battery Sign*, his
was an apocalyptic vision.

REDEMPTION BY BEAUTY: ROMANTIC FORM

Like the English romantics, Williams loved lyric poetry. Like them, he
adored Shakespeare, but unlike most of the playwrights of the great ages
of romanticism, he did not restrict his theatre to poetic closet dramas. It
is a tribute to Williams's genius that, in spite of his romanticism, he was
able to craft plays that were meant for the stage.

He blended the melodramatic form of the nineteenth century with contemporary realities, counterbalancing the exuberant hyperbole with ironic litotes. Thus Blanche DuBois can wear her feather boa, but Stanley Kowalski, in his undershirt, will sneer at her pretenses at "royalty." A grand old actress, like the Princess Alexandra del Lago, can demand and command, but she knows that she is pathetic rather than tragic, pretentious rather than real. Their exotic names, their large gestures, their taste for rhetoric and overwrought scenes place them solidly in the grand style of the romantics. Yet Williams was enough of a realist to acknowledge their faults, to undercut their theatricalism with irony, but he loved to produce them for our entertainment.

In a beautiful letter to Brooks Atkinson (Key West, 2TLS, "June 7 or 8, 1953"), Williams expressed his gratitude to this faithful old critic for understanding his vision of the theatre. Atkinson, the *New York Times* reviewer, was one of the few who understood what *Camino Real* was really about and expressed his disappointment at its weak reception. Williams insisted that it was written as a "communion with people." "Preserving it on paper isn't enough," he said, "a published play is only the shadow of one and not even a clear shadow. The colors, the music, the grace, the levitation, the quick inter-play of live beings suspended like fitful lightning in a cloud, those things are the play, not words, certainly not words on paper and certainly not any thoughts or ideas of an author, those shabby things snatched off basement counters at Gimbel's." He then goes on to refer to the speech in *The Doctor's Dilemma*, of which he can no longer remember a line. But he does remember that, when he heard it, he thought, "Yes, that's what it is, not words, not thoughts or ideas, but those abstract things such as form and light and color that living things are made of." One of his most lacerating letters in response to a critic was written when Williams thought that Walter Kerr had missed all of the music, color, dance, and theatricality of *Camino Real*. He had missed "the great plastic richness" and the consequent demands on the whole troupe of performers and practitioners. (A copy of the letter, unsigned, undated, and probably unsent, is in the Billy Rose Theatre Collection at Lincoln Center.)

Given Williams's romantic rejection of traditional controls and forced conventions, it is hardly surprising that he would have espoused this dynamic form.[25] From his earliest critical comments, printed as a preface to *The Glass Menagerie*, Williams rejected the realistic theatre with its fourth-wall conventions. His letters are full of passionate pleas to actors, directors, producers not to subvert the poetry of his plays. He had a vision of the theatre as lively painting, poetry in motion; he loved color, dance, and music. Although he mentioned his admiration of Aristotelian form—especially the unities—he felt no compulsion to conform to classic or neoclassical principles of dramaturgy. He preferred to explore his own patterns. Like Pirandello, he was fascinated by the process of perception, the multiple meanings of reality. He enjoyed underscoring the primary role of the artist by showing the dreamer as well as the dream. In *Camino Real*, Don Quixote introduces his vision of the Royal Road that has become the Real Road. Tom Wingfield explains that *The Glass Menagerie* is a "memory" play and that the memory is his.

Perhaps it was an element of his basic comedic view of life that brought this doubleness to his drama. Like Shakespeare with his plays-within-plays, Williams liked to set the narrator outside the drama, thereby allowing an ironic counterpoint to the melodrama of the tale. Tom, like the artist, stands inside the story and outside it simultaneously. Inside, his voice is personal—angry and loving; outside, it is analytic—it is dry and ironic. At the beginning of *The Glass Menagerie*, the Narrator-Tom presses the audience to see the story as a part of the world picture; later he draws attention to himself as a Stage Magician; and finally, he demands our sympathy as he leaves the doomed women to blow from place to place like leaves from Shelley's "Ode to the West Wind." Like other framing devices that Williams used in early plays, the Narrator underscores the play as a play, a presentational device designed to disorient the audience.

Williams's experiments in presentational drama—*Camino Real* as Don Quixote's dream, *Battle of Angels* as a memory play set in a museum, *Out Cry* as the fragment of a clouded memory being reconstructed as it is acted and viewed—were challenges to the popular realistic play with its fourth-wall convention. Williams pressed the artist's "God-like freedom" in the act of creation, able to destroy the illusion at will by calling attention to it as an illusion.[26] This acting-out of the role of the Promethean rebel-as-artist continued to the extent of deconstructing the play as it is being presented. This climaxed in *Out Cry*, where the characters tease out the different levels of illusion and reality as they suffer through their genuine distress.

This fiction of non-control, which is the mark of romantic irony, produces a work riddled with unresolved ambiguities, in which the artist creates a sense of his own inability to master his recalcitrant materials.[27] Thus, we watch Felice-the-actor worrying about the absence of the production crew, Felice-the-character involved in the action of the play, and Felice-the-writer arguing with Clare about the actual events from which the play derived. At the end, the deliberate decision to reenter the world-of-the-play in order to escape the world of the make-believe-theatre is painfully ironic and clearly ridiculous, but somehow right. As Furst notes, without grounding in external reality, we enter the hall of mirrors, "plunged into the persona's paradoxes, ambivalences, ironies, and schizophrenic dualisms..." (33). Williams-the-relativist welcomes this opportunity to force the audience to join him in the curious quest of the romantic, ultimately a quest of the imagination. His imagery of the legless bird is a fitting symbol of the artist who rejects the solid grounding in reality. The flight ends only with death.

The life on stage was for Tennessee Williams an image of the human condition, not simply a chronicle of individual experience. His was a mythic vision, involving people with allusive names, performing ritual actions in the "circle of light." Taking his cue from the Church, he transformed the stage into an altar and the play into a ritual. He allowed no limits on the creator-artist or his claims for his prophetic role. It is no wonder he wrote of that "visionary company." For him, no human was more valuable, on earth or in heaven, than the Artist.

In those last plays, the poetry diminished, the experience of life dimmed, the characters pressed into pitiful choices. But like the Ancient Mariner, the compulsive old playwright continued to fix us with his glittering eye and tell us his compelling tale of the voyage, the violation, the pain, and the aching hunger to expiate his sin. His hands no longer seemed so blessed, his message grew blurred, he saw more of life as ugly, but he never lost faith in the redemptive power of beauty.

As the sweet bird of youth finally flew out of sight, and Williams grew to be an "old alligator," in letters to friends he insisted that he was still a romantic—though now a senile one.[28] One of the saddest pieces of writing in the Harvard Collection is an unfinished letter to the actors in what he called his "last long play for Broadway," asserting that this play was "intransigently romantic." He concluded by saying that, though now an old man, he still responded to the "cry of the players." (1TLS, N.P., N.D.)

NOTES

1. The phrasing is from Shaw's play *The Doctor's Dilemma*, quoted in Tennessee Williams, "Afterword to *Camino Real*," in *Where I Live: Selected Essays* (New York: New Directions, 1978), 69.

2. See, for example, the letter from Tennessee Williams to Audrey Wood, 2TLS, Laguna Beach, CA, June, 1939, in which he identified himself with Vachel Lindsay and provided a lengthy description of a proposed script (Harry Ransom Humanities Research Collection—hereafter HRHRC—University of Texas, Austin).

3. Lillian Furst, *The Contours of European Romanticism* (Lincoln: The University of Nebraska Press, 1979), 3.

4. Tennessee Williams to Audrey Wood, 3TLS, NP [Probably Laguna Beach, CA], May 5, 1939. HRHRC, Austin.

5. Albert J. Devlin, ed., *Conversations with Tennessee Williams* (Jackson, Mississippi: University Press of Mississippi, 1986).

6. This rough draft document entitled "The Visionary Company" is part of the Williams collection at HRHRC, Austin, Texas. I have silently corrected some typographical errors.

7. Lyle Leverich, *Tom: The Unknown Life of Tennessee Williams* (New York: Crown, 1995), 44, describes Senator John Sharp Williams, who was noted for his comic stories as well as his rhetoric.

8. "Preface to My Poems," in *Where I Live: Selected Essays*, I (reprinted from *Five Young American Poets*).

9. See the discussion of Blake and the other romantics in Lawrence S. Lockridge's *The Ethics of Romanticism* (Cambridge University Press, 1989), 22 ff.

10. It is interesting that Lyle Leverich constructs his impressive work in terms of a romantic search, entitling chapters: "Lodestar," "Moonward," "Outer Space," "Wanderings," and "New Harbors." All of these are images of the journey, a standard romantic image.

11. Tennessee Williams to Audrey Wood, 1TLS, Nantucket, July 29, 1946. HRHRC, Austin.

12. This is a different play from the later *Fugitive Kind*, a version of *Battle of Angels*. New Directions plans to publish several of these early plays within the next few years.

13. Alan Ehrenhalt, *The Lost City: Discovering the Forgotten Virtues of Community in the Chicago of the 1950's* (New York: HarperCollins, 1995).

14. Tennessee Williams, "Home to Key West," in *Where I Live*, 160.

15. See *Hart Crane and the Image of the Voyage*, a work which reveals any number of parallels to Tennessee Williams's life and thought.

16. Tennessee Williams's letters to Margo Jones (in the HRHRC, Austin) in the mid-sixties already mention his regular reading of these authors. Jay Laughlin sometimes shipped him boxes of books that were his own favorites. In return, Williams sent Laughlin materials on Crane, including biographies he thought interesting. (The Laughlin letters are soon to be published at New Directions.)

17. Janet Maslin, in a review of *Total Eclipse*, entitled "Rimbaud: Portrait of the Artist as a Young Boor," in the *New York Times*, November 3, 1995, C–14. Maslin notes that Rimbaud is the source of much contemporary popular culture, including Bob Dylan, Jim Morrison, and Patti Smith.

18. For a full description of Mishima's romanticism, see Susan Jolliffe Napier's *Escape from the Wasteland, Romanticism and Realism in the Fiction of Mishima Yukio and Oe Kenzaburo* (Cambridge, MA: Harvard University Press, 1991).

19. Allean Hale has discovered a "secret" Noh play that Williams wrote as a tribute to Mishima. Williams referred to "The Mutilated" as a "Yes Play" in one typescript version in the Billy Rose Theatre Collection.

20. He thanked Donald Windham for the gift of wind chimes and mentioned them in letters to others as well.

21. See, for example, Lyle Leverich's account of the room in which he lived when he first moved to Key West and lived at the Trade Winds, or Allean Hale's description of the papers she discovered to be his "Secret Manuscript," a Noh Play.

22. See letter from TW to Robert MacGregor, March 27, 1963, in the New Directions Archive.

23. Tennessee Williams to Audrey Wood, 3TLS, from Tangiers, October 14, 1953 HRHRC, Austin.

24. Tennessee Williams to Audrey Wood, 1TLS, from Nantucket, July 29, 1946. HRHRC, Austin.

25. René Welleck, in *Concepts of Criticism*, speaks of the romantics' use of dynamism, organic form, and change. See Furst, 8.

26. Furst, 27.

27. Furst, 31.

28. Tennessee Williams to Oliver Evans, 1TLS, from Rome, July 10, 1971. The Houghton Library at Harvard University.

BIBLIOGRAPHY

Abrams, Mark. *The Mirror and the Lamp*. London: Oxford University Press, 1953.

Barzun, Jacques. *Romanticism and the Modern Ego*. Boston: Little, Brown, 1944.

———. *Classic, Romantic and Modern*. Garden City, New York: Doubleday, 1961.

Bate, Walter Jackson. *From Classic to Romantic*. Cambridge: Cambridge University Press, 1946.

Combs, Robert. *Vision of the Voyage: Hart Crane and the Psychology of Romanticism*. Memphis State University Press, 1978.

Cranston, Maurice. *The Romantic Movement*. Oxford: Blackwell, 1994.

Driver, Tom. *Romantic Quest and Modern Query*. New York: Delacorte Press, 1970.

Furst, Lillian R. *The Contours of European Romanticism*. Lincoln: University of Nebraska Press, 1979.

Lovejoy, Arthur O. *The Great Chain of Being. A Study of the History of an Idea*. New York: Harper & Row, 1936.

Praz, Mario. *The Romantic Agony*. New York: The World Publishing Co. 1933.

SIGNI FALK

The Literary World
of Tennessee Williams

I. A New Concept of Theater

Tennessee Williams was thirty-four when *The Glass Menagerie* acclaimed him as a new voice, and he was thirty-six when *A Streetcar Named Desire* broke theatrical records. For Williams, theater offered a medium for giving the audience an emotional experience, for exploring the inner mechanisms of human personality and behavior, and for doing so in a way that might be startling or shocking but forceful enough to be remembered. In his determination to reach across the footlights, he has made use of the old theatrical devices that have been effective in popular drama over the centuries; but he has also exploited the endless possibility of technology to add new ones. As a result, he has returned excitement to the theater.

He is said to have "changed the theater and the taste of the theater" and to have opened the way in America for dramatists who, like Pinter, have explored the complex and hidden psychological drives that motivate people. In Williams' continuing presentation of themes previously considered untouchable; of derelicts and misfits, outcasts from a materialistic society; and of the thin line between sanity and insanity, he has revealed a broken world not often portrayed. Because of his bent toward sensationalism, he might seem to have escaped from the

From *Tennessee Williams*. © 1978 by Twayne publishers. Reprinted by permission.

realistic tradition dominated by Ibsen and Shaw that continued with the
Group Theater, a tradition that viewed the stage as a kind of lecture hall
or pulpit. However, because of Williams' preoccupation with the ugly
world in which monsters and hypocrites destroy the defeated, frustrated
little people, he has given much of his work the quality of morality plays.

II. WRITING AS AUTOBIOGRAPHY

From the beginning, whatever Tennessee Williams wrote was a record
of his own experience that is sometimes directly, sometimes obliquely
stated. Williams himself is a highly complex person who has admitted
that he has not written anything that he has not known firsthand, that
what he finds in himself at the time of writing he assumes to be universal
experience, and that he believes in the "absolute one-ness" of the artist
and his work.

As has been observed earlier about Williams, his childhood bout
with diphtheria restricted his activities and his acquaintance with normal
children, drove him to books and his own fantasies, lengthened his
dependence on his mother and led to his early estrangement from his
father, and developed a lifelong hypochondria over his health in spite of
his doctor's assurances. The intense personal commitment to his sister,
Rose, the alter ego of his childhood whose mental crisis was so tragically
mishandled and without his knowledge, has continued throughout his
life; for years he has supported her in a sanitarium at Ossining, New
York. It has been said "that the curtain came down with the loss of Rose."
She, who never should have been subjected to the rigors of a Southern
debut, and whose sexual fantasies shocked the mother, was subjected to
one of the earliest and least expensive experiments in prefrontal
lobotomy.

As Williams grew older, he understood the incompatibility
between his strict and at times unworldly mother and his father, who was
a boisterous Cavalier but at heart "a totally honest man." He understood
why his father found his relaxation in drinking and poker, and why he
was distressed by the growing effeminacy of his son. When Williams
could do so financially, he enabled his mother to secure a divorce, but he
felt sympathy in the later years for this man of difficult temper who was
relegated to a lonely hotel room where he died alone. To Williams'
friends, he is in a way his father's own son: he is boastful of his

masculinity, unafraid of a confrontation, and for years was a notable drinker and poker player.

Though devoted to his mother, he later referred to his "infantile impotence" as a writer as a consequence of his pampered childhood; and his changing attitudes may be reflected in his increasingly bitter characterizations of mothers. This figure in his writing represents the strictures and morality inherited from the Puritans that have been hardened into a few simplistic rules. Garrulous Amanda, for all her set ideas of goodness, is sympathetically presented; but Mrs. Buchanan in *Eccentricities* is a dominating mother and a fool; Big Mama is silly and coarse. The later works also seem to imply that the mother prevented the normal development of her son: the mother in "Mama's Old Stucco House," the mother described by the Reverend Shannon, and most despicable, Mrs. Venable of *Suddenly Last Summer*. Williams has referred to his own mother as "that slightly cracked southern belle," and he has implied that her "sum total influence" led him into homosexuality. About her verbal compulsion, he observed recently that his mother will "be talking a half hour after she's laid to rest."

Camden or Clarksdale, Mississippi, towns where he lived happily with his grandparents, came to represent the "vanished Eden" and Southern gentility at its best. In contrast to these idyllic scenes of his childhood, he discovered as a young adult the French Quarter of New Orleans where he became a "confirmed Bohemian." The conflict between these two meaningful experiences—the proprieties of his early training and the unlimited freedom discovered in New Orleans— perhaps helps to account for the extremes of his own reaction and for the subsequent direction of his own life. This conflict is reflected in the sense of guilt that hounds the "immoralists" in his stories and plays, for they are tormented by having indulged in their deviations. The shock of the bohemian freedom and his pleasure in it may also have supported his early conviction that no subjects are taboo for a writer.

III. PREOCCUPATION WITH SEX

There has always been in Williams a quaint absorption in the old-time Puritan preoccupation with sex, the sin that Dante placed at the rim of hell since it is far above and less despicable than fraud and deceit. In the earliest plays, he portrays sexual freedom as a kind of "redemption" that is available only to women and in comic situations. It becomes a panacea for the women in "The Crushed Petunias" and in *You Touched Me!*; it is a glorious indulgence in "Yellow Bird" and "Miss Coynte of Greene"; and it apparently "resurrects" Serafina delle Rose in *The Rose Tattoo*, the raped girl in *27 Wagons*, Myrtle in *Seven Descents*, and Dorothy in *Period of Adjustment*. In other cases, sex takes the form of perversion: Blanche and Alma represent "corrupted innocence," as do Val Xavier and Chance Wayne and, to a worse degree, Mrs. Stone. Williams' paean to male sexual vigor is to Stanley Kowalski, but he also praises Latin lovers like Vacarro and Alvaro. The young doctor in *Summer and Smoke* seems like a parody of Stan.

In the early writing of Williams, disguised references are made to homosexuality or to a contrast between the attractive homosexual and an obnoxious "normal" character. When the subject became commonplace, Williams described the relationship with increased particularity. The poem "San Sebastiano de Sodoma" is a glowing tribute to the saint-homosexual in ambiguous terms. "Night of the Iguana" and "Two on a Party" take a defensive attitude to the theme, and Blanche's husband is a victim of social rejection. "Rubio y Morena" cloaks the theme in the seemingly transvestite character of the large Mexican girl. Baron de Charlus, in *Camino Real*, justifies himself as escaping from the sordid world; Brick Pollitt is also an escapist. Apollo of "One Arm" is favorably contrasted to the host and his guests at the stud party, and the writer-narrator-Williams in *Moise and the World of Reason* elaborates upon his pleasure with Lance, the black ice skater. Sebastian in *Suddenly Last Summer* is a degraded figure. The dude, Quentin, of *Small Craft Warnings*, complains about the dreary monotony and loss of sensibility in the homosexual. The old men, gallery habitués in "Hard Candy" and "The Mysteries of Joy Rio," and the ancient who pursues the writer in *Moise*, are pitifully depraved figures. Williams' sympathy with sexual abnormality in later years has given way to a compulsion to tell all about himself and his world. He knew that his *Memoirs* would bring "considerable embarrassment" to his publishers, but he refused "to dissimulate" the facts of his life.

IV. The Sensitive and the Predatory

Williams has always placed his protagonist, a sensitive and lonely individual of either sex, in an unfriendly world. The poet-itinerant-outsider—the male who is often closely identified with his creator—seeks to avoid the full responsibilities of a job and of family life. The protagonist can be recognized as Williams throughout his work: he appears in the early poems; he is the young lumberman in *Moony's Kid Don't Cry*; he is Tom Wingfield, who ran away from home and the shoe factory but could not forget Laura; he is Val writing a book on life; he is Chance Wayne, a failed artist who like Val is aware of the enemy time, fleeting youth, and imminent death; he is the son in "Mama's Old Stucco House"; he is Christopher Flanders, who eases rich old women into death. The outsider thinks of the creative force as a kind of vision: Val Xavier, Vee Talbott, Mark in *Tokyo Bar*, and Moise. The outsider may be a former athlete, like Kilroy or Brick; he may be an idealist or an innocent; he may be the one-armed Apollo—but all are marked by the "charm of the defeated." Williams first achieved recognition for his delineation of the feminine outsiders, Southern gentlewomen, moth figures destroyed by predators, who appear in the stories "Portrait of a Girl in Glass," "Portrait of a Madonna," "Three Players of a Summer Game," and "The Night of the Iguana." These gentlewomen, "trapped by circumstance," later appear as Amanda Wingfield and her daughter Laura, as Blanche Du Bois, as Alma Winemiller, as Isabel Haverstick, and as Hannah Jelkes.

The predators, the destructive mammoth figures, take several forms: Stanley, the primitive sexual force; the symbols of power and seedy corruption in *Camino Real*; The Gooper clan in *Cat*; the rednecks in *Battle of Angels* and *Orpheus*; Boss Finley and his son Tom in *Sweet Bird*; the black therapist in "Desire and the Black Masseur"; the starving children in *Suddenly Last Summer*. The predator may be a dominant woman like the rich and decadent Mrs. Stone; the rich, moribund Flora Goforth; the Princess Kosmonopolis; Mrs. Faulk, the aggressive padrona in *Iguana*; or Mirium in *Tokyo Bar*.

Tennessee Williams has said that he is unable to create normal characters, but a few stand out: Stella Kowalski, happy with her husband; Nellie, the giggling teenager in *Summer and Smoke*; Baby Doll, a bit addlepated but attractive; Maggie the Cat, scrapping for her share in life;

Catharine Holly, with her passion for truth telling; Serafina's daughter, with her healthy view of sex. Among the men are Jim O'Connor, who struggles for self-improvement; John Buchanan in *Eccentricities*; Mitch, who is devoted to his mother but is also an acceptable partner at poker; Scudder, a kind of haberdasher's model who courts Heavenly Finley. The salesman of the solid gold watches is the integrity of the old order, and Big Daddy, a full-blooded, self-made man, is a materialist who is as perceptive as he is rich.

V. WILLIAMS AS SCENEWRIGHT

Williams, always concerned with highly charged dramatic scenes rather than with organic development, has been called "a vivid and exciting *scene* wright." Individual scenes often represent Williams at his theatrical best. Among many examples are the following: the delicately renewed acquaintance between Laura and Jim; the violent erotic clash between Blanche and Stanley; the courtship scene between Serafina and the new truck driver; the comedy scene of Baby Doll protecting her virtue; part of the Brick–Big Daddy argument; the confrontation of Lady and David Cutrere; the dramatic truth telling of Catharine Holly; the confessional Hannah–Shannon scene.

The Glass Menagerie, which in form is as simple as a short story, is very effective; and the same assessment might be made of *Eccentricities of a Nightingale*. Williams' habit of overloading characterization is paralleled often by multiplying discordant plot elements and by including too much of everything. *Battle of Angels* and *Orpheus Descending* are complicated by extraneous characters and universal meanings; *Summer and Smoke* and *Sweet Bird of Youth* also attempt too much; and, after two good acts, *The Rose Tattoo* and *Cat* are artificially concluded in a weak third.

The Glass Menagerie has been called a series of one-act plays, and the same could be said of *Camino Real*. The clash between two people in one scene or act may be repeated in the following one but with different characters, as in the first and second acts of *Cat* or the two scenes of *Suddenly Last Summer*. The episodic construction lends itself to the memory technique: *The Long Goodbye* preceded its full use in *The Glass Menagerie*. The techniques of delayed bit-by-bit confession make up the early one act, *The Dark Room*; a series of self-revelations unfold the story of Blanche; the story of incest in *The Purification* is revealed piecemeal; *Small Craft Warnings* is almost entirely a series of recollections, as is *Period of Adjustment*.

VI. Idiomatic Language

When at his best, Williams conveys the impression of idiomatic language, no matter how different the mood and subject. Critics from the beginning have noted the clever way he combines clichés and original speech. Through his use of words, he has been able to increase suspense and to enhance the quality of character and emotion. He has added dramatic intensity by delaying revelations during the dialogue, as in *Cat*; he develops the entire situation in *This Property Is Condemned* in casual dialogue; he substitutes dramatic argument for action in the later plays, as in *In the Bar of a Tokyo Hotel* and in *Out Cry*. He often concludes an explosive argument with a quiet line: Big Daddy's answer to Big Mama, the doctor's quiet comment after the story in *Suddenly Last Summer*. Unfortunately, Williams has not been able to strike from his plays those rhetorical lines that on occasion hold up a scene. Sometimes lines of self-conscious poetry, of pseudophilosophy, or of schoolmaster's exposition intrude upon the attention. At times characters deliver long speeches or arias, as Elia Kazan called them. As noted earlier, Joseph Wood Krutch, reviewing the opening of *The Glass Menagerie*, spotted this weakness and urged the young playwright to strike any line that he particularly liked.

VII. Experimental Devices

Because Williams has had a definite idea of what theater should be, he has experimented with many devices and theatrical techniques to enhance the dramatic impact of his plays. He often sets one scene against another. While Blanche sings in her bath, Stan unravels her ugly story; when Blanche appeals to Mitch, the Mexican woman is calling "*Flores para los muertos*"; when Blanche at the phone attempts to contact a former suitor, a drunk and a prostitute struggle off stage. When Rosa pleads for love with Jack, noisy off-stage sounds tattle on Serafina and Alvaro. The ugly squabble over the estate in *Cat* is accompanied by Big

Daddy's cries of agony; the *pieta* scene with the Madrecita and Kilroy and the post mortem one occur simultaneously in *Camino Real*—unfortunately; the busy second act of *Sweet Bird* contrasts off-stage brutality with Chance Wayne "frozen" on stage.

Williams has resorted to symbols, some effective and some not; he justifies their use as "the purest language of plays" and as a short cut that eliminates tedious exposition. The little glass ornaments belong to Laura; the snakeskin jacket seems to represent Val's freedom; the trunk of faded dresses and letters in the crowded apartment suggests Blanche and her intrusion. The bird imagery in *Orpheus* and *Suddenly Last Summer* seems literary, and the fountain and the anatomy in *Summer and Smoke* seem forced; *The Rose Tattoo* is cluttered with roses, goat cries, and eccentrics. Other symbols are obvious: A. Ratt, and the plane Fugitavo in *Camino*; the big double bed and the television set in *Cat*; the confectionary in *Orpheus*. Many characters are symbols, and for some reason the degenerates—Blanche, Apollo, and Sebastian—appear in white. When Mrs. Stone represents the corruption of our time, poor Kilroy every little struggling man, or the predicament of Chance Wayne a commonplace, the symbolism then belongs to the private world of the playwright.

To intensify the mood, Williams makes full use of light and color as if he himself were a painter. The vivid poker game in *Streetcar* is likened to a Van Gogh picture; the setting for *Summer and Smoke* is to resemble the nonrealistic design of a Chirico; *The Rose Tattoo* calls for blue sky like that in an Italian painting of the Renaissance. Like the mood music of the films, sound enriches many of Williams' scenes: the cheap music across the alley in *Menagerie* suggests Americans unaware of the Spanish Civil War; the community band in the city park in *Summer and Smoke* conveys an age gone by; the jungle noises in the mad scenes in *Streetcar*, and repeatedly throughout *Suddenly Last Summer*, heighten the tensions; the "blue piano" underscores the sexual theme in *Streetcar*.

VIII. WILLIAMS' COMIC SENSE

From the beginning, Williams has shown a talent for comic figures and scenes: the outlandish and amusing riffraff in the poems; Archie Lee Meigham, who builds his own humiliation; the silly tourists in *Lord Byron's Love Letter*; the preposterous McGillicuddys in *Period of*

Adjustment; the clumsy salesman in *Tattoo*; the gossiping wives in *Battle of Angels*; Billy Spangler, yes man in "The Knightly Quest"; grotesques like the Gooper "no-neck monsters"; the garish Rosa Gonzales in *Summer and Smoke*; the stately witch in *Milk Train*; the impertinent youth in *Gold Watches* and *Portrait of a Madonna*; a clutch of ministers—the Lutheran in "One Arm," and the several reverends in the plays.

Williams' comic sense emerges in several scenes in *The Glass Menagerie*: Amanda's trying to sell subscriptions, the lights going out on the dinner party, Jim's trying out his speech lessons on Laura. There are comic scenes in *Streetcar*: Blanche's outlandish pretensions, Stanley's explanation of the Napoleonic Code, his frustrations over her condescension. Williams can spin a humorous yarn: "The Yellow Bird," "Miss Coynte of Greene," most of "27 Wagons Full of Cotton," and the situation revealed in the play *The Dark Room*. He shows his talent for folk comedy in the ribald humor of Alvaro's courtship of the widow; her discovery of Rosario's infidelity and acceptance of the new truck driver. His bent for satire is evident in such scenes as the literary evening in *Summer and Smoke*, or in the character of Braden Gewinner in "The Knightly Quest."

Often, the public may not share Williams' sense of the comic: his own laughter at *Suddenly Last Summer*; the intended humor of *Period of Adjustment*; the rape of the fat girl in *27 Wagons* and "Knightly Quest"; the cruel laughter in *Gnädiges Fräulein*. The quick flash scenes of a naked or near-naked woman—Carol Cutrere, *Battle of Angels*; Eve, *Camino Real*; Mrs. Goforth, *Milk Train*—may be funnier than the playwright intended. Kenneth Tynan has commented on Williams' "mental deafness" that makes him laugh in the wrong places.

IX. PORTRAYAL OF EVIL

His contemporary world is often a kind of hell: the small towns in *Battle of Angels* and *Orpheus* destroy the outsider representing the virtues of the Old South; racist Jake in *27 Wagons* burns the Italian's mill and exploits black labor; in the hell of *Camino Real* the individual is expendable; St. Cloud, in *Sweet Bird*, is dominated by a racist brand of gestapo; the town in "The Knightly Quest" is a government-operated police state. As indicated, the death motif is closely allied with the predator theme: the everpresent Streetcleaners in *Camino Real*; the Val Xaviers are persecuted by the sex envious; atonement in *Suddenly Last Summer* takes the form of cannibalism; the death theme permeates every character in *Sweet Bird. Iguana* and *Milk Train*, with an emphasis on acceptance of the inevitable, represent a turning point.

Williams exploited the dramatic possibilities of the Easter story: the devouring of little Anthony Burns culminates on Good Friday; Val Xavier is crucified by a blow torch on Saturday night before Easter; Chance Wayne is castrated on Easter Sunday. Williams has his own interpretation of Christ as the savior of mankind: Apollo of "One Arm" takes the confessions of participating homosexuals, as if he were Christ; Val Xavier becomes the image of Christ for Vee Talbott; Christopher Flanders becomes a Christ figure with an Oriental slant; and, in the incredible final scene of *Moise and The World of Reason*, narrator-Williams, whose feet the artist Moise bathes and wipes with her own hair, seems to personify Christ. The references to God, as if in human form, emerge in even stranger images when the Reverend Shannon blames God for his faulty construction of the universe; Doc in *Small Craft Warnings* speaks of God as a sightless black man; in the same play, Violet's God apparently exists in her lecherous fingers; little, luckless Kilroy pities everybody, the world, and even God Who made it.

X. WRITING AS THERAPY

From the time that Williams was twelve years old, so he has repeatedly said, writing has been a therapy for him, a "purification" of sickness. Often the work that appears after an illness or a traumatic experience reflects a jaded view of a world that is full of monsters and of "enormous hypocrisy." Williams has admitted that it is easier for him to identify with those "who verge upon hysteria." As one critic wrote, Williams' view of life is "always abnormal, heightened and spotlighted and slashed with bogy shadows." His affinity with the disenchanted and with the drug cults has raised questions as to whether or not he was a spokesman for the vocal subculture of the 1960s. Though he denies that his work is autobiographical, the many interviews of recent years, the "psychological dissections," and the *Memoirs* indicate the very close parallels between his work and his own life.

XI. THE PRICE OF EARLY SUCCESS

Fighting to regain the high position he achieved early in his career with a play about every two years, Williams has subjected himself to merciless criticism when he has been unable to reach his audience. His reaction to these rejections and subsequent illnesses have become part of the public record. Claudia Cassidy suggested that Williams, who was able to create "many valorous characters," was perhaps too vulnerable to bring that same valor into his own life; that the violence in his plays came from within him; that he rewrote to meet directors' demands; that he let himself be injured by unfavorable criticism. Sometimes Williams' multiple revisions suggest that he does not trust his own judgment, or that, as he has admitted, the revising delays the separation between him and his work at hand.

His hard and dedicated labor has earned him both prestige and money. In 1962 Williams was reputed to have earned over six million dollars in his playwriting career, though he does not consider himself in the material class with Terrence Rattigan or Noel Coward. His firsthand experience with theatrical business has sharpened his sense of what should come his way; his later plays reflect a bitterness against those who have exploited him, and he has been his own best publicist. For years, a piece always appeared in the *New York Times* preceding the opening of a play. His absentmindedness about money is legendary, but so is his generous support of writers and artists who need encouragement.

XII. AMBIGUITY ABOUT HONESTY

Williams has always valued honesty above morality. He praised the honesty of his father and of his long-time companion-secretary, Frank Merlo; the honesty of Alma in *Eccentricities*, of Brick and Maggie in *Cat*, of Catharine in *Suddenly Last Summer*. Whether the demands of honesty in *Memoirs* exist to quiet his own soul or to make the book a best seller remain ambiguous. And yet if an interviewer, having made the conditions clear beforehand, writes about the "hermetic atmosphere" and the "Byzantine complexities" of Williams' Key West establishment, the playwright dashes off a mad letter to the editor.

There has crept into the later works a vulgarity and a coarseness that is not to be found in the early stories and one acts but that may be

included because it has become necessary to "hit them with something."
Although one critic called Williams "a gentleman who seethes with
inner violence and something akin to self hatred," Williams, except for a
few pieces, continues to be preoccupied with sex, about which he is not
only explicit but also startling in vocabulary. The soft images of early
childhood and the tender feelings for the unfortunate are strangely
mixed with the kind of expressions that suggest the graffitti of an early
teenager who is thumbing his nose.

Success has brought problems. For years an itinerant like his
protagonists, but known worldwide in later years, Williams has had to
battle for privacy. Quite early he became suspicious of praise: "I'm afraid
I often think they are trying to make a fool out of me." A man of volatile
temperament and one who is scrappy when his work is attacked, he can
be abusive; but, having tasted the bittersweet fruits, he is able to be
"reasonably objective about himself." He told Mike Wallace that "all
reputations in the theater are inflated reputations," and that no one is as
good as the publicity suggests. He added wryly that, as the discrepancy
between the actual being and the public image widens, the reputation
increases. He recognizes that the sex theme is no longer startling, that
his "pseudo-literary style" is on the way out, and that his own *bête noir*
has been his tendency to poeticize. He continues to be much interested
"in the presentational form of theater, where everything is free and
different, where you have total license."

XIII. WILLIAMS' POSITION IN THE AMERICAN THEATER

As Brooks Atkinson wrote in 1956 after seeing a revival of *The Glass
Menagerie*, "To see it again is to realize how much he has changed. There
is a streak of savagery in his work now. The humor is bitter. The ugliness
is shocking. He has come a long way since 1945—growing in mastery of
the theater, developing power, widening in scope. He has also renounced
the tenderness that makes 'The Glass Menagerie' such a delicate and
moving play." Louis Kronenberger, apropos of *Sweet Bird*, commented
on the development of the playwright: "Whether a world of loathing and
disgust, or sex violence and race violence, of lurid and bestial revenges,
constitutes Mr. Williams' personal reaction to life or simply his
philosophic vision of it, it has come to seem compulsive in him rather
than convincing in his people." The often pilloried Claudia Cassidy has

asked what happened to this playwright "whose talent for lyric theater was streaked with laughter"; to his "intuitive sense of direction"; and to his plays that have become monstrous."

Stanley Kauffmann paid tribute to the playwright whom all actors want to play: his "superb theatrical talent; his eye for stage effect, his skill in scene construction, his gift for dialogue that can cut to the bone, that can use cliché with humor and poignancy, and that can combine the odd floridness of lower class character with his own rich rhetoric." Disappointed in Williams' later work in which Kauffmann finds an increasingly thinner disguise of old material, he observes that what was shocking in former years is later only "tame and self-consciously squalid." He also notes that what formerly was considered "sexual candor" and "poetic evocation" has now "taken on taints of merchandizing for the Williams market." Kauffmann recommended, as has been noted earlier, that Williams exploit his great talent for "outrageous comedy."

Williams continues to write and to rewrite, and producers continue to mount his plays on American and foreign stages. It is obvious that the playwright is trying to work with a variety of dramatic forms and to exploit changing techniques in order to reach his audience, but he has not very successfully done so in his more recent years. *Vieux Carré* (1977), a restatement of old material in a form reminiscent of *The Glass Menagerie* (1945), is, like *Out Cry* (1959), a static play in the Chekhovian tradition. According to reports, *Red Devil Battery Sign* (1975) combines an incredible plot with political implications; another play of the 1970s, *Whore of Babylon*, is said to be "outrageously funny"; and *This is (Entertainment)* (1975) deals with the funny side of social revolution.

Williams, generally recognized as the foremost playwright to have emerged in the American theater, has for over three decades dominated not only the stages of his own country but also of the international theater. Walter Kerr, who has always been ready to recognize the touch of genius in an otherwise poor Williams' play, has repeatedly proclaimed that his contribution has been considerable. In his latest statement, part of his review of *Vieux Carré*, Kerr acknowledges that "our best playwright ... has already given us such a substantial body of successful work that there is really no need to continue demanding that he live up to himself, that he produce more, more, more and all masterpieces." He recommends that Williams' public gratefully tuck into the portfolio "the casuals ... as small dividends." Walter Kerr—and this writer agrees—believes that the stature of Tennessee Williams has become so well established that, as a playwright, he does not need to wait for the judgment of future generations.

Chronology

1911	Born in Columbus, Mississippi.
1911–18	Lives with mother and sister in grandparents' home, moving often.
1918	Family moves to St. Louis.
1927	First story published in Smart Set magazine.
1928	Visits Europe with grandfather; story published in Weird Tales magazine.
1929	Enrolls at University of Missouri, Columbia; wins honorable mention for play, *Beauty Is the World*.
1932	Father pulls him out of school for flunking ROTC.
1935	Hospitalized for exhaustion, visits grandparents in Memphis where his play *Cairo! Shanghai! Bombay!* is produced.
1935–37	Enters Washington University, St. Louis; enters University of Iowa; first full-length plays produced, *Candles to the Sun* and *The Fugitive Kind*; lobotomy performed on sister, Rose.
1938	Graduates from University of Iowa.
1939	Receives Rockefeller grant.
1940	To New York; attends playwriting seminar.
1941–43	Begins *The Gentleman Caller* (later *The Glass Menagerie*); works at MGM as a scriptwriter.

1944	*The Glass Menagerie* opens in Chicago.
1945	*The Glass Menagerie* opens in New York; receives New York Critics' Circle Award.
1947	*A Streetcar Named Desire* opens in New York; *Summer and Smoke* opens in Dallas; wins Pulitzer Prize.
1948	*Summer and Smoke* opens in New York; *American Blues: Five Short Plays* published; *One Arm and Other Stories* published.
1950	*The Roman Spring of Mrs. Stone*, a novel, is published.
1951	*The Rose Tattoo* opens in New York; film version of *A Streetcar Named Desire* released.
1953	*Camino Real* opens in New York.
1954	*Hard Candy*; A Book of Stories published.
1955	*Cat on a Hot Tin Roof* opens in New York; wins Pulitzer Prize.
1956	*Baby Doll* film is released.
1957	*Orpheus Descending* opens in New York; father dies; Williams begins psychoanalysis.
1958	*Something Unspoken* and *Suddenly Last Summer* open Off-Broadway; film version of *Cat on a Hot Tin Roof* released.
1959	*Sweet Bird of Youth* opens in New York.
1960	*Period of Adjustment* opens in New York.
1961	*The Night of the Iguana* opens in New York; receives New York Critics' Circle Award.
1962	Film version of *Sweet Bird of Youth* is released.
1963	*The Milk Train Doesn't Stop Here Anymore* opens in New York; Frank Merlo dies.
1964	Film version of *The Night of the Iguana* is released.
1966	*Slapstick Tragedy* opens in New York.
1968	*Kingdom of the Earth* opens in New York.
1969	*In the Bar of a Tokyo Hotel* opens Off-Broadway; Williams converts to Roman Catholicism; spends three months in a hospital after nervous collapse.
1970	*Dragon Country*: A Book of Plays is published.

1971	*Out Cry* opens in Chicago.
1972	*Small Craft Warnings* opens Off-Broadway.
1973	*Out Cry* opens in New York.
1974	*Eight Moral Ladies Possessed*: A Book of Stories is published.
1975	Receives the National Arts Club gold medal for literature; *Moise and the World of Reason* is released; *The Red Devil Battery Sign* opens in Boston; Memoirs are published.
1976	*The Red Devil Battery Sign* opens in Vienna.
1977	*Vieux Carre* opens in New York.
1978	*A Lovely Day for Creve Coeur* opens in Charleston, South Carolina; *Where I Live: Selected Essays* is published.
1979	*A Lovely Day for Creve Coeur* opens in New York.
1980	*Clothes for a Summer Hotel* opens in Washington, D.C.; mother dies.
1981	*A House Not Meant to Stand* opens in Chicago; *Something Cloudy, Something Clear* opens in New York.
1982	Receives honorary degree from Harvard University.
1983	Dies on February 24/25 in New York.

Works by Tennessee Williams

Not About Nightingales, 1938.
Battle of Angels, 1945.
The Glass Menagerie, 1945.
Twenty-Seven Wagons Full of Cotton & Other One-Act Plays, 1946.
A Streetcar Named Desire, 1947.
You Touched Me!, 1947 (With David Windham).
American Blues: Five Short Stories, 1948.
One Arm and Other Short Stories, 1948.
Summer and Smoke, 1948.
The Roman Spring of Mrs. Stone, 1950 (Novel).
I Rise in Flame, Cried the Phoenix, 1951.
The Rose Tatoo, 1951.
Camino Real, 1953.
Hard Candy: A Book of Stories, 1954 (Short story collection).
Cat on a Hot Tin Roof, 1955.
Baby Doll, 1956.
In the Winter Of Cities, 1956 (Poems).
The Fugitive Kind, 1958.
Orpheus Descending, 1958.
Suddenly Last Summer, 1958.
Garden District, 1959.
Sweet Bird of Youth, 1959.
Period of Adjustment, 1960.
The Night of the Iguana, 1961.

Eccentricities of a Nightingale, 1964.

Grand, 1964.

The Milk Train Doesn't Stop Here Anymore, 1964.

The Knightly Quest: A Novella & Four Short Stories, 1966.

Kingdom of Earth, 1967.

The Mutilated, 1967.

Two-Character Play, 1969.

Dragon Country, 1970.

Out Cry, 1973.

Small Craft Warnings, 1973.

Eight Mortal Ladies Possessed, 1974 (Short story collection).

Memoirs, 1975.

Moise And The World Of Reason, 1975 (A Novel).

Eccentricities of a Nightingale, 1976.

Androgyne, Mon Amoiur, 1977 (Poems).

Where I Live: Selected Essays, 1978.

Vieux Carre, 1979.

A Lovely Sunday for Creve Coeur, 1980.

Something Cloudy, Something Clear, 1981.

Clothes for a Summer Hotel: A Ghost Play, 1981.

In Masks Outrageous and Austere, 1983.

Works about Tennessee Williams

Adler, Thomas P. "Before the Fall—and After." *The Cambridge Companion to Tennessee Williams*, ed. Matthew C. Roudane. New York: Cambridge University Press, 1997, 114–127.

———. "Tennessee Williams's 'Personal Lyricism': Toward an Androgynous Form." *Realism and the American Dramatic Tradition*, ed. William W. Demastes. Tuscaloosa: University of Alabama, 1996.

Asibong, Emmanuel B. *Tennessee Williams: The Tragic Tension*. Ilfracombe: Stockwell, 1978.

Bigsby, C.W.E. "Entering *The Glass Menagerie*." *The Cambridge Companion to Tennessee Williams*, ed. Matthew C. Roudane. New York: Cambridge University Press, 1997, 29–44.

Bloom, Harold, ed. *Tennessee Williams*. Modern Critical Interpretations. New York: Chelsea House Publishers, 1988.

Boxill, Roger. *Tennessee Williams*. Modern Dramatists. London: Palgrave Macmillan, 1989.

Clum, John M. "The Sacrificial Stud and the Fugitive Female." *The Cambridge Companion to Tennessee Williams*, ed. Matthew C. Roudane. New York: Cambridge University Press, 1997, 128–146.

Cohn, Ruby. *Dialogue in American Drama*. Bloomington: Indiana University Press, 1971.

Day, Christine R., and Bob Woods, eds. *Where I Live: Selected Essays by Tennessee Williams*. New York: New Directions, 1978.

Debusscher, Gilbert. "Tennessee Williams as Hagiographer: An Aspect of Obliquity in Drama." *Revue des Langues Vivantes* 40 (1970): 449–456.

Devlin, Albert J. *Conversations with Tennessee Williams.* Jackson: University Press of Mississippi, 1986.

Donahue, Francis. *The Dramatic World of Tennessee Williams.* New York, F. Ungar, 1964.

Falk, Signi Lenea. *Tennessee Williams.* Boston: Twayne, 1962, 2d ed. 1978.

Fedder, Norma J. *The Influence of D.H. Lawrence on Tennessee Williams.* The Hague: Mouton, 1966.

Fleche, Anne. *Mimetic Disillusion: Eugene O'Neill, Tennessee Williams, and U.S. Dramatic Realism.* Tuscaloosa: University of Alabama Press, 1997.

Griffin, Alice. *Understanding Tennessee Williams.* Columbia, South Carolina: University of South Carolina Press, 1994.

Hayman, Ronald. *Tennessee Williams: Everyone Else Is an Audience.* New Haven: Yale University Press, 1993.

Jackson, Esther Merle. *The Broken World of Tennessee Williams.* Madison: University of Wisconsin Press, 1965.

Leavitt, Richard F. *The World of Tennessee Williams.* London: W.H. Allen, 1978.

Leverich, Lyle. *Tom: The Unknown Tennessee Williams.* New York: Crown, 1995.

Londré, Felicia Hardison. *Tennessee Williams: Life, Work, and Criticism.* Fredericton, New Brunswick: York Press, 1989.

Magical Muse: Millennial Essays on Tennessee Williams. Tuscaloosa: University of Alabama Press, 2002.

Martin, Robert A, ed. *Critical Essays on Tennessee Williams.* New York: Simon & Schuster, 1997.

Maxwell, Gilbert. *Tennessee Williams and Friends.* Cleveland: World, 1965.

Nelson, Benjamin. *Tennessee Williams: The Man and His Work.* New York: Ivan Obelensky, 1961.

Pagan, Nicholas. *Rethinking Literary Biography: A Postmodern Approach to Tennessee Williams.* Cranbury, New Jersey: Fairleigh Dickinson University Press, 1993.

Rader, Doston. *Tennessee: Cry of the Heart*. Garden City, New York: Doubleday, 1985.

Rogers, Ingrid. *Tennessee Williams: A Moralist's Answer to the Perils of Life*. Frankfurt am Main: P. Lang, 1976.

Saddick, Annette J. *The Politics of Reputation: the Critical Reception of Tennessee Williams' Later Plays*. Madison, New Jersey: Fairleigh Dickinson University Press, 1999.

Spoto, Donald. *The Kindness of Strangers: The Life of Tennessee Williams*. Boston: Little, Brown, 1985.

Thompson, Judith J. *Tennessee Williams' Plays: Memory, Myth, and Symbol*. New York: P. Lang, 1987.

Tischler, Nancy Marie Patterson. *Tennessee Williams*. Austin, Texas: Steck-Vaughn, 1969.

———. *Tennessee Williams: Rebellious Puritan*. Citadel Press, 1961.

Weales, Gerald Clifford. *Tennessee Williams*. Minneapolis, University of Minnesota Press, 1965.

Williams, Dakin, and Shepherd Mead. *Tennessee Williams: An Intimate Biography*. New York: Arbor House, 1983.

Williams, Edwina Dakin. *Remember Me to Tom*. New York: Putnam, 1963.

Williams, Tennessee. *Five O'Clock Angel: Letters of Tennessee Williams to Maria St. Just, 1948–1982*. New York: Knopf: Distributed by Random House, 1990.

———. *Mémoirs*. Garden City, N.Y.: Doubleday, 1975.

———. *The Selected Letters of Tennessee Williams*, eds. Albert J. Devlin and Nancy Tischler. New York: New Directions, 2000.

———. *Tennessee Williams' Letters to Donald Windham, 1940–1965*. New York: Viking, 1980; Athens, Georgia: University of Georgia Press, 1996.

Windham, Donald. *Lost Friendships: A Memoir of Truman Capote, Tennessee Williams, and Others*. New York: W. Morrow, 1987.

Websites

The Tennessee Williams/New Orleans Literary Festival
www.tennesseewilliams.net/

American Masters – Tennessee Williams
www.pbs.org/wnet/americanmasters/database/williams_t.html

Mississippi Writer's Page: Tennessee Williams (1911–1983)
www.olemiss.edu/depts/english/ms-writers/dir/williams_tennessee/

Perspectives in American Literature: Tennessee Williams (1911–1983)
www.csustan.edu/english/reuben/pal/chap8/williams.html

The Tennessee Williams Annual Review
www.middleenglish.org/tennessee/twar/twar.htm

The Tennessee Williams Page
www.lambda.net/~maximum/williams.html

Contributors

HAROLD BLOOM is Sterling Professor of the Humanities at Yale University and Henry W. and Albert A. Berg Professor of English at the New York University Graduate School. He is the author of over 20 books, including *Shelley's Mythmaking* (1959), *The Visionary Company* (1961), *Blake's Apocalypse* (1963), *Yeats* (1970), *A Map of Misreading* (1975), *Kabbalah and Criticism* (1975), *Agon: Toward a Theory of Revisionism* (1982), The *American Religion* (1992), The *Western Canon* (1994), and *Omens of Millennium: The Gnosis of Angels, Dreams, and Resurrection* (1996). *The Anxiety of Influence* (1973) sets forth Professor Bloom's provocative theory of the literary relationships between the great writers and their predecessors. His most recent books include *Shakespeare: The Invention of the Human*, a 1998 National Book Award finalist, and *How to Read and Why*, which was published in 2000. In 1999, Professor Bloom received the prestigious Gold Medal for Criticism from the American Academy of Arts and Letters.

NORMA JEAN LUTZ has been writing professionally since 1977. She is the author of more than 250 short stories and articles as well as 40-plus books—fiction and non-fiction.

A recent graduate of Pennsylvania State University with an MFA in Fiction, AIMEE LABRIE has published stories in journals such as *Beloit Fiction*, *Pleiades*, and *Scribner's Best of the Fiction Workshop* and book reviews in *CALYX* and *Willow Springs*. She works as a freelance writer and lecturer in English at Penn State and is revising her first novel.

NANCY M. TISCHLER, Professor Emerita of English at Pennsylvania State University, is the author of the first critical study of Williams' work, *Tennessee Williams: Rebellious Puritan*, the first critical study of Williams's work. She has co-edited, with Albert J. Devlin, *The Selected Letters of Tennessee Williams*.

SIGNI FALK was a professor emerita of English at Coe College. Her writings include books on Tennessee Williams and Archibald MacLeish. Falk served on the Iowa advisory committee to the U.S. Commission on Civil Rights (1972–1982) and on a White House committee on the elderly in 1981.

INDEX

NOTE: In all cases, Williams without a modifier refers to Tennessee Williams. An "*n*" following a page number indicates an endnote.